ROCKHOUNDING
New York

A Guide to the State's Best Rockhounding Sites

ROBERT BEARD

FALCONGUIDES

GUILFORD, CONNECTICUT
HELENA, MONTANA
AN IMPRINT OF GLOBE PEQUOT PRESS

To buy books in quantity for corporate use
or incentives, call **(800) 962-0973**
or e-mail **premiums@GlobePequot.com**.

FALCONGUIDES®

FalconGuides is an imprint of Globe Pequot Press.
Falcon, FalconGuides, and Outfit Your Mind are registered trademarks of Morris Book Publishing, LLC.

All photos by Robert D. Beard unless otherwise noted.
Maps by Daniel Lloyd © Morris Book Publishing, LLC.

Text design: Sheryl P. Kober
Layout: Sue Murray
Project editor: Ellen Urban

Library of Congress Cataloging-in-Publication Data is available on file.

ISBN 978-0-7627-7900-0

Printed in the United States of America

10 9 8 7 6 5 4 3 2 1

CONTENTS

Atlantic Coastal Plain

Manhattan Prong

Hudson Highlands

Overview

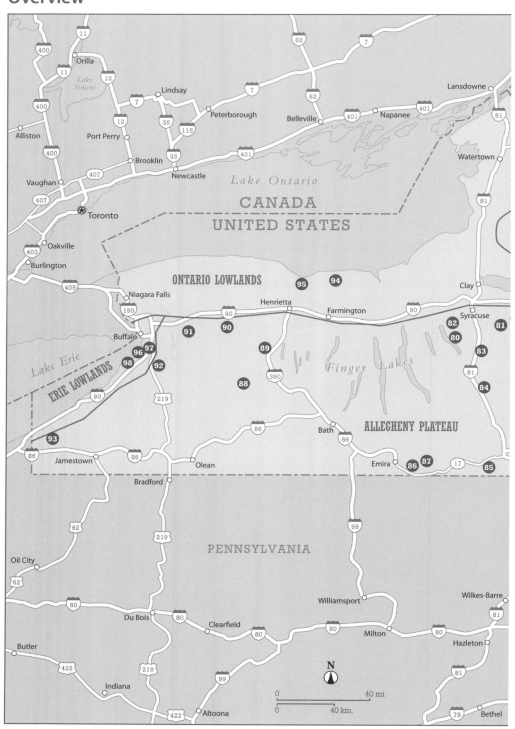

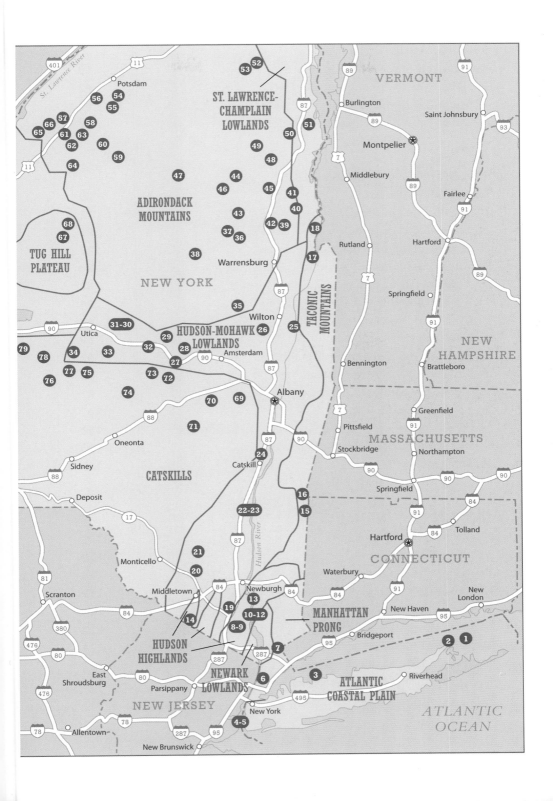

Taconic Mountains

Hudson-Mohawk Lowlands

Adirondack Mountains

Ontario Lowlands

Erie Lowlands

ACKNOWLEDGMENTS

Many people have helped make this book possible. I would first like to thank my editor at *Rock & Gem* magazine, Lynn Varon, who put me in contact with Globe Pequot Press, and William Kappele, another Rockhounding series writer and contributing editor at *Rock & Gem,* who suggested me to Lynn as a potential author for Globe Pequot in 2011. My writing experience with *Rock & Gem* enabled me to learn much more about rock, mineral, and fossil collecting than I ever anticipated.

I would like to thank my editors at Globe Pequot Press, David Legere, and Ellen Urban, for their patience when I had numerous delays due to inclement weather, and Melissa Baker in the map department, who gave me extremely helpful comments and suggestions. Thanks are also due to the production staff and the many people who were instrumental in producing and distributing the book.

Before doing field research for *Rockhounding New York,* I came across many websites, blogs, and forums that gave excellent information on potential sites and often provided key information that enabled me to find difficult-to-locate sites. Although I have met some providers of this Web information at mineral shows, most have no idea how important their information was to this book. Among these Web authors, special thanks go to John Betts, Jeff Wilson, Michael Walter, and Dr. Karl Wilson from the State University of New York in Binghamton.

Other online sources that should be acknowledged are the New York State Geological Association, the Rochester Academy of Science, Friends of the Grenville, the New York State Museum, the Penfield Foundation Museum, and Mindat.org. Their websites, online guidebooks and conference proceedings all provided invaluable information.

In addition to online sources, I also benefited greatly from numerous printed articles on New York minerals by authors such as Dr. Steven Chamberlain of the New York State Museum and Dr. George Robinson of Michigan Tech. Many of these were published in *Rocks & Minerals* and the *Mineralogical Record.*

On a more personal note, I am also grateful for all the help I received from staff and managers at the fee-collecting sites that I visited: the Penn-Dixie

Quarry, Herkimer Diamond Mines, Ace of Diamond Mines, Crystal Grove Mines, Diamond Acres, and the Barton Mines. I also want to express my appreciation to the Garnet Hill Lodge for allowing me access to the Hooper garnet mine, and to the many helpful individuals I met at the sites mentioned who shared their knowledge and provided various levels of assistance. If any of them by chance read this book, and remember our meeting, thank you for your help.

Lastly, I would like to thank my wife, Rosalina, and my children, Daniel and Roberta. They came on some key trips and endured many long drives despite being past the age when going on trips is involuntary. While they often now choose not to come on field trips, I hope they will look back on those trips in the positive way Rosalina and I do. For us they are among our best memories.

INTRODUCTION

This book is geared toward that rockhound or geologist who wants to visit sites without significant advance arrangements. Virtually every type of rock-collecting trip can be found in this book. Some sites will allow you to park your car and pick up rocks as soon as you get out. Other sites require some walking, and some sites require a lot of strenuous hiking over bad terrain. In some, you'll likely find lots of minerals, and in others, you may have to work hard to find anything. Some sites have minerals that you can grab with your bare hands, and others will require you to use a sledgehammer to extricate them from host rock. In each case, I have done my best to help you easily find these sites and let you know what to expect.

New York is one of the first states where mineral collecting became popular, and the state also has some of the oldest mines in the United States. While New York has a wide variety of mineral occurrences, as in much of the East, many of these are on private land or public sites where mineral collecting is prohibited. In fact, there's been an increase lately, readily apparent in reviewing online information, toward private sites becoming public ones, whether as parklands or preserves. Other traditional collecting sites around mines have also been closed to collectors due to environmental contamination. Still, there are a wealth of collecting sites still open to the interested rockhound and a good many where even studying the rocks and recording them in photographs or video makes for a great outing and educational adventure.

In this book I have focused on identifying such sites where people can visit by themselves or with their family without significant advance planning or permission. Within this group, I have included fee-collecting sites that allow visitors to search for Herkimer diamonds, garnet, and other minerals as well.

In researching sites for the book I found that access could be a major challenge. Surprisingly, roadcuts were nearly always accessible, providing you could find safe parking. On the other hand, collecting along lakesides and beaches was often a problem as much of the waterfront land is private. Property maps that I obtained online were often of limited value. I have seen property marked as private that is accessible, and property marked as public that is often posted.

It is imperative to obey all signs and obtain permission to access off-limit areas. Just because a site is described in this book does not mean it will remain accessible or that collecting is permitted on the site. I have personally checked every one of the sites in this book. Many of the sites are roadcuts, roadside "borrow pits," or outcrops that are somewhat limited in size but are reasonably accessible for visitors. Roadcuts are often within the highway right-of-way and sometimes belong to the state or local government. Generally you can collect in these areas if they are safe and you are not disrupting traffic, but I have also heard that roadside collecting may be illegal in New York. For what it is worth, I have never had a problem, but I always make certain that I am not inside posted ground and that I am not in an area where I am posing a risk to traffic.

Interstate highways are also illegal collecting sites, and I am aware of some mineral occurrences along New York interstates that are referenced in other texts that I kept out of this guide for that reason. There are few feelings that are more discouraging than being at a site and having a police car pull up behind you, especially if you know you are not supposed to be there. Of course, land and access status can change at any time. Even if a private site is not posted, this guide does not imply or suggest that collecting at the site is permitted.

Many entries in this book are in county parks, state forests, state parks, federal lands, or other places that are accessible to the public, and while you can go to these sites, rock collecting is prohibited in many of these locations. However, rock-collecting rules are not applied uniformly in many cases. If you look at the park regulations you will generally find that any form of ground disturbance, which technically includes simply picking up a rock, is strictly prohibited. However, many of these same parks and New York universities often publish field guides to these parks. In these cases you will have to use your best judgment as to whether or not you are going to collect rocks if you visit a site. If there are signs clearly stating "no mineral collecting," do not collect rocks. Likewise, if you are in a place where you know collecting is forbidden, you can look at the rocks, but do not collect them. Good examples of these types of sites where collecting is prohibited are the stromatolites at Lester Park and the pillow basalts at Starks Knob, which are New York State Museum Educational sites. Often it is best to preserve the rocks for future visitors, especially if removing or hammering the rocks will damage the outcrop.

Where an interesting mineral or fossil occurrence is on publicly accessible land, but collecting is prohibited, I have still listed it in this book if I have been able to visit it and consider the locality worthy of a visit by anyone interested in rocks. Despite the efforts of some regulators I have not yet found a site where it is against the law to look at the rocks.

As mentioned earlier, you'll find key fee-collecting entries in this book. These are well worth visiting, despite the admission expense, which may be relatively small when you compare them to the cost in gas and time to get to the site. At these sites, minerals and fossils are generally easy to find and parking and access are nearly always available.

I have stayed away from listing mine and quarry sites where you have to obtain advance permission and appointments, as many rockhounds often do not have the ability to schedule and make advance arrangements. Quarries and mines are generally best visited as a group with a local mineral club or other organization. Such group trips to quarries could be well worth your time, as you'll bypass identifying landowners and permission issues, but you must also make sure that you bring your own hard hat, steel-toed boots, hammer, and other tools that might be appropriate for the rock types you may encounter. For the rockhound with family members who don't love rocks quite as much as you do, this book also includes local attractions near each site. Many of these are local state parks, nearby lakes, and, in urban settings, nearby malls and cities. These should help you plan a trip that's fun for everyone. New York is a very big state, and it is nearly impossible to cover every locality. While I attempted to include as many sites as possible in this book, I found that the list of good sites kept growing, and eventually I had to draw the line on adding additional ones. The good news is that the more I kept looking, the more sites I kept finding. This is important, as it shows that there are still more sites to visit. I have never run out of potential places for looking at rocks. This book may be a good starting point in finding your own "hidden" site.

The best way to learn about rock collecting is to go out and look for rocks. You and your companions are bound to see some interesting geology and scenery too as you experience the adventure of going on a field trip, even if just for a morning or afternoon.

ROCKHOUNDING BASICS

Rockhounding can be a low-budget hobby, especially when you are just starting out, as the entry requirements are relatively minimal. All you need are your eyes and hands to see and pick up interesting rocks. However, as you advance you'll want some additional tools.

Collecting Equipment

A good **hammer** is the most important tool for a rockhound. I recommend a rock pick hammer with a pointed tip. Hardware stores don't usually carry these, but they are available at some surveying supply shops, at rock shows, and online. My preferred brand is an Estwing, foot-long hammer with a pointed tip and a Shock Reduction Grip. I have used mine for over thirty years. It is almost impossible to destroy, despite thousands of whacks against very hard rocks and lots of time outside in the rain and snow.

Do not use a regular claw hammer. These will break apart quickly, and the steel that shoots off the hammer head when it hits a rock can be very dangerous. If you are hammering, it is also critical to wear safety glasses or goggles. I wear glasses normally to see, and my glasses have often been damaged by flying rock chips and steel. In the event that I am hammering large rocks on a constant basis, such as in a quarry, I will cover my glasses with safety goggles. When collecting in urban environments, rocks are often associated with broken glass, which becomes another hazard when hit with a hammer. I also use a chisel to help break apart rocks when needed, but many chisels have very wide blades and are difficult to use when splitting the soft finely bedded sediments that are common in many fossiliferous shales. I sometimes use a cheap flat-bladed screwdriver for soft shaly rocks where a chisel is too big to use. I know this is not the proper use of a screwdriver, but I have not found a better tool for splitting apart soft shaly rocks. Of course, if you try to use a flat-bladed screwdriver to split apart hard rocks, you are abusing the tool and run the risk of breaking the screwdriver or injuring yourself. In a case where you are splitting harder rocks, your best tool will likely be a chisel, and you may need to find one with a very narrow blade if the rocks must be split along very tight fractures.

Gloves are the next critical item. In the old days I used to do fieldwork without gloves, but realized quickly that it was a dangerous practice. Make sure you protect your hands. All of us with day jobs that require the use of a computer are in big trouble if we temporarily lose the use of a finger or hand. Get a good pair of heavy leather work gloves from your local hardware or big box store. You will also find that gloves are great when moving through briars, climbing on sharp rocks, and avoiding broken glass. It is also extremely easy to pinch your bare fingers when moving around large rocks, but gloves will help prevent the pinching. It is far better to get the end of your glove caught under a rock than the tip of your finger.

Get a good pair of steel-toed or equivalent **boots** to protect your feet. Having steel-toed boots is a requirement for collecting in quarries and mines, and it is very easy to find and purchase a good pair. I prefer to have relatively lightweight boots. Be sure to walk in them before purchasing to find a pair that fits comfortably.

A **hard hat,** while not needed for collecting at most roadcuts or places without overhead hazards, is equipment you should always have readily available. While you may not need one for casual rock collecting, you should have one with you or in your car in case you get invited to collect in a quarry or visit an active mine.

A **field book** and **camera** are also very useful for recording key site information. I like to record coordinates of sites and take notes of what I have found for future reference. I also use a small pocket-size digital camera and often take hundreds of shots a day to increase my chances of getting that perfect shot. A **hand lens** to inspect mineral and fossils up close is also very useful. I recommend getting a quality hand lens that is at least 10X magnification.

Carrying your rocks from the site is often a chore. I like to use a small **backpack** when I have to walk a long distance, but sometimes a five-gallon plastic bucket works best. A bucket is useful when you are picking up muddy rocks, and it is easy to put in your car. Just be careful to not break the bottom of the bucket if you intend to also use it for water. I have ruined several buckets with large, sharp rocks.

A **wagon** is also good to have if you are working in quarries or places where you can expect to take out significant amounts of rocks. If you go on a trip with a mineral club to a quarry, you can always tell who knows what they are doing, as they often come with a wagon to haul the rocks out of the pit. Collecting lots of rocks in a quarry is fine, as what you do not collect is just going to go to a crusher. However, if you go on a trip to an outcrop or small site and need to bring a wagon, you are collecting way too many rocks. Be considerate, and save some for the next visitor.

GPS Units and Maps

Before digital mapping, I used to find every site by using topographic and highway maps, but those days are long over. I now use a handheld Global Positioning System (GPS) unit to record key site location information, and I use the coordinate feature on my car GPS to take me to the site. I still meet people who are not using all available features of their GPS unit, such as the latitude and longitude feature, so be sure you brush up on all the available features of yours. Many rockhounds don't have this dedicated device, but rather use their smartphone GPS app. My GPS is still separate from my phone, and I like to record my locations by hand. However, I have used a smartphone in the field and found the satellite imagery, combined with real-time tracking, was very helpful for finding difficult-to-locate sites. If you do not use a GPS at all, I strongly recommend that you start, either with a dedicated device or an app. Keep up with advances in mapping technology too, as newer and better navigation methods will likely keep coming.

Despite the advantages of GPS units and smartphones, you should always have maps as a backup. I like to have a state map, and I often get free maps at rest areas. I have also found my standard US road atlas works very well. Batteries can die, and satellite and mobile signals can be dropped in wilderness and urban areas where you do not have good clearance for satellite signals. Sometimes your charger will also short out, which happened to me in northern New York, and I suddenly felt like I was traveling blind. A good highway map can also be a relatively simple check for your GPS unit.

If possible, you should also get topographic maps of your site. I used to buy hard-copy maps, but they are relatively expensive, especially when you are looking at several sites. I recently bought set of topographic maps on CDs from National Geographic, but unfortunately they have discontinued the CD series and replaced them with online maps. I found these to be completely unsuitable for my purposes, as I am often in areas without online access. I am hoping that technology and Internet access will improve to the point where I will access online topographic maps, but for now I am still working with my older copies on CD.

Health and Safety

Rockhounding presents many hazards that you will not encounter in other hobbies. In addition to having the proper gear, there are many health and safety considerations. Any time you go into the field, you are going into an uncontrolled and potentially hostile environment, and you need to take some basic steps to protect yourself and your collecting companions.

Sunscreen is one of the most effective and easy-to-use safety products, but many collectors still ignore its benefits. However, you need to put it on right away after you get to the site, or even better, before you leave the house. Many sites, especially the floors of open pit mines, act like giant solar reflectors, and the sun can be very intense. I also highly recommend a good pair of dark sunglasses. I cannot spend any time at all in an area of light-colored rocks if I do not have my sunglasses. Likewise, if you are not wearing a hardhat, wear a baseball cap or other hat for protection from the sun.

Although sun is often an issue, rain is also a big issue in New York. I highly recommend having an umbrella handy. I know it sounds ridiculous, but I have gone on many extended hikes in the woods in driving rain with an umbrella, and this helped a great deal. As long as there is not lightning, an umbrella can make a big difference in the quality of your trip.

Poison ivy can be a serious problem in New York. If you do not know how to recognize poison ivy, you will become an expert after you get your first serious rash. Poison ivy usually grows on the borders of outcrops and rocks, and this is another good reason to wear gloves. In fact, if your gloves have had extensive contact with the poison ivy, you may just have to throw them away.

While I always enjoy collecting in shorts and short-sleeve shirts, many sites are hidden among briars and other plants that can make your experience miserable if your legs and arms are exposed. I recommend always having a pair of long pants and a light jacket available if you need it, and you can also anticipate that these clothes will get ripped by thorns, broken branches, and sharp rocks. Long pants and sleeves can also help protect you from the sun and insects as well as flying rock chips from hammering.

Ticks are a major concern in the northeastern United States. I usually find that I have been exposed to ticks as I am driving away from the site and see several crawling on my arms and legs just as I am entering traffic. There is no worse countermotivation for a young or new rockhound than going home covered in ticks, and while hell hath no fury like a woman scorned, watch what happens if your wife or daughter finds a tick. Lyme disease is a serious issue, and you have to be on your guard at all times. The larger wood ticks, while not aesthetically pleasing, are typically not carriers of Lyme disease, while the much smaller deer ticks are known carriers. If you find a small tick embedded in you, and it has been there for more than twenty-four hours, you may be at risk for Lyme disease. Keep an eye on the bite mark and contact your physician if it gets worse over the next few days. Using an insect repellant that contains DEET is a good defense, as is light-colored clothing so you can quickly spot and remove the ticks. Insect repellant is also good to keep away the mosquitoes, which may be present at any sites near standing water. To remove a tick, grasp the skin around the insertion of the tick with a pair of fine-point tweezers and pull straight outward; be careful not to grasp the tick body as it may inject germs into the skin. Even with insect repellent you can still get bit. I received a lyme tick bite this summer, and had a bright red circle on my shoulder almost immediately. My doctor put me on antibiotics and apparently this took care of it, but I never even saw the tick.

I recommend an orange or yellow safety vest if you are collecting near a roadside. Roads will always be dangerous, and many of the sites in this guide are at roadcuts. Provided you park in a safe place and stay well off the road, you should not have a problem, and the safety vest may alert cars to your presence.

Dehydration and hunger are trip spoilers. Make sure that you and your collecting companions bring enough bottled water, and if you will be out all day, bring something to eat. Nearly all of the sites in this guidebook are near cities and places where you can get lunch, and most trips are half-day trips, so hunger is generally not a problem. Water, on the other hand, can be a problem. I generally have at least one half-liter of bottled water in my backpack and often take two half-liters of bottled water, and make sure that my collecting companions also have bottled water. I know this sounds obvious, but it is not a good situation to be miles from the car and not have water for a thirsty person whom you have introduced to rockhounding. Never, ever drink water from a mountain stream, no matter how remote or how good it looks, unless you are equipped with a proper filter.

Getting to the site safely is important. The parking areas for the sites in this book can all be easily reached with a two-wheel-drive vehicle. It seems obvious, but if you are driving to a site, be sure your vehicle will get you there, and that you have plenty of gas. I always try to keep my tank topped off. I found that gas stations are relatively easy to find in New York, but I do not like it when my tank gets low. If you are taking more than one vehicle, make certain that there will be enough parking for two cars. Many drives are also very long, so if you get tired, be sure to pull over at a secure rest area and take a break.

While many collecting sites are in somewhat rural areas, some of the sites in this book are in urban settings. You should always be aware of your surroundings, make sure your vehicle is parked in a secure place, keep your vehicle GPS hidden, do not leave valuables visible in your car, and be alert for suspicious characters. Generally if you have a bad feeling about where you parked your car, you will find that feeling has been justified when you return.

Underground mines are generally a non-issue in New York, as most of the unstable mines collapsed or were closed many decades ago, and many of the open mines now have bat gates or other structures that keep people out. However, it is still possible to come across open portals and shafts, especially in the magnetite mining districts of southern and northern New York. The best policy is to stay outside of any underground workings.

Finally, you have to be careful when dealing with sites on private property. Always ask permission if you can, and be prepared to get yelled at or have other unpleasant experiences with landowners. Many of my most unpleasant experiences have involved dealing with their large and quite vicious dogs. Nearly all owners I have talked with have been good about giving permission, but every now and then I come across unfriendly owners. This challenge comes with the hobby, so if you are going to look for rocks on private lands and ask their owners for access, you have to be ready to deal with difficult people.

Important Online Tools

Many mineral and fossil localities have recently disappeared into developments, yet in that same timeframe it's become much easier to find new sites. Google, Yahoo, Google Earth, and Google Maps all can be accessed to identify sites and explore potential localities.

I have purposely left website addresses and phone numbers out of this guide, as Internet addresses often expire, and phone numbers change, and generally it is much easier to find a Web address via a search engine. Running an Internet search on a locality often brings up new and potentially important information updates, especially if a site has changed land status.

Likewise, all of the references cited in this book refer to the actual publication and do not provide a web address for access. However, if you type in the citation or key parts of it, you can often access them online. If not, you can generally get them through your state library. I have found that many publications are now only available on microfiche, but your librarian can often arrange for a copy to be e-mailed to you.

NEW YORK GEOLOGY

Some basic understanding of the geology of New York will help you understand why you encounter certain rocks, minerals, and fossils in various parts of the state. New York is a large state and has considerable variation in its geology, and nearly all rock types and geologic periods are represented to some extent.

New York can be roughly divided into ten geologic provinces. These are the Atlantic Coastal Plain, the Manhattan Prong, the Hudson Highlands, the Newark Lowlands, the Taconic Mountains, the Hudson-Mohawk Lowlands, the Adirondack Mountains, the Tug Hill Plateau, the St. Lawrence-Champlain Lowlands, the Allegheny Plateau, the Ontario Lowlands, and the Erie Lowlands.

Atlantic Coastal Plain
In New York, this province includes Long Island and a small portion of Staten Island. It is a continuation of the coastal plain physiographic province that extends along the eastern United States to the Gulf of Mexico. Long Island is underlain by Cretaceous, Tertiary, and Quaternary sediments that gently dip towards the Atlantic Ocean. The only significant bedrock exposures in Long Island are Cretaceous sediments that form many of the shoreline cliffs along the northwestern section of the island. Hematitic and limonitic concretions, which are often called "Indian paint pots," are found in these sediments. The beaches, especially in the eastern section of the island, often are covered with coarse pebbles of quartz, feldspar, and other reworked granitic and metamorphic rocks.

Manhattan Prong
The Manhattan Prong covers the area of Manhattan and extends northeast into Westchester County. It is a complex of metamorphic rocks that range in age from Precambrian to Lower Ordovician. Some of the key formations include the Fordham Gneiss, Manhattan Schist, and Inwood Marble. The rocks have been folded and faulted, and many exposures have significant glacial striations. The basement rocks are very hard and durable and formed an excellent base for the buildings of Manhattan. Many excellent mineral localities were found when the rocks were first excavated for the subway, water tunnels, and

buildings, but many of these same localities are now covered by concrete and asphalt. However, it is still possible to see the rocks in the numerous parks that dot the area, and interesting minerals can sometimes be found in the dumps of excavated rocks from the tunnels and other construction projects.

Hudson Highlands

The Hudson Highlands are some of the region's oldest rocks. They consist of metamorphic rocks that originally formed the Grenville Mountains, but they were ultimately eroded and now form the Hudson Highlands. Many of the first iron mines of the United States were in the Hudson Highlands, and many of these mountains are now state forests. Many of the scenic hiking trails in the Highlands lead to some of these former iron mines.

Newark Lowlands

The Newark Lowlands is the area between the Manhattan Prong and the Hudson Highlands. This is a terrain with relatively low relief, and it formed from layers of igneous and sedimentary rocks that were deposited during the Triassic-Jurassic period. The Palisades Sill, which is a classic New York feature, occurs within the Newark Lowlands.

Taconic Mountains

The Taconic Mountains, which lie east of the Hudson River, were formed from massive slices of crust that were thrust onto the area from the east. These were further pushed together when a volcanic island arc collided with the edge of the continent during the Taconic Orogeny. The sedimentary rocks of these mountains are generally Cambrian and Ordovician sandstones and shales. Metamorphism of some of these shales also resulted in a belt of slate, but the slate deposits are just over the New York border and in the states to the east. Some of the mineral deposits in the Taconic Mountains that are in New York include iron and graphite.

Hudson-Mohawk Lowlands

The Hudson-Mohawk Lowlands cover the Hudson River Valley and Mohawk River Valley. These lowlands are formed from soft sedimentary rocks that are more readily eroded than some of the more resistant rocks of the surrounding area. These are mainly lower Paleozoic sediments, including limestones, dolomites, and shales. Many of the limestones are fossiliferous, and some of the Cambrian-age dolostones contain Herkimer "diamonds" in the Mohawk Valley area. Many streams and other features in the Hudson Valley and nearby regions end in the word "kill," which is from the Middle Dutch word *kille,* which meant riverbed or water channel. If you see a geographic feature in southern New York with "kill" in the name, it often is related to a water feature. The Hudson and Mohawk valleys were important transportation routes in the early days of New York and many of the important population centers of upstate New York remain within these valleys.

Adirondack Mountains

The Adirondacks are a large, roughly circular region of deeply weathered Precambrian rocks. Unlike many mountain ranges that are bounded by faults or other relatively sharp boundaries, the Adirondacks were formed by a broad uplift that brought the Precambrian rocks near the surface, and the overlying sediments have long been stripped away. Satellite photos show that the rocks have rough northeast-southwest and east-west patterns that resemble fractures, and many of the key drainages formed along these patterns. The Adirondacks are a major tourist attraction for upstate New York and much of the economy in the region is based on tourism. The soils are poorly suited for agriculture, and the rough topography also makes farming and rural life very difficult. The Adirondacks had many important iron and zinc mines, and garnet, wollastonite, and talc were also mined. Many of these mines have long since closed, but some of the garnet and wollastonite mines are still active.

Tug Hill Plateau

The Tug Hill plateau is a relatively small province that is elevated with respect to the surrounding Ontario Lowlands province. The region is underlain by Middle and Upper Ordovician carbonate and clastic rocks. The area is a relatively undeveloped part of New York, based on looking at a New York highway map. Although it is flat, it technically is not a plateau, as the sedimentary rocks that form its core areas are tilted. The area is known for the heavy snowfall it receives as a result of its location just east of Lake Ontario. Over 200 inches of snow fall on the region each year. The Tug Hill plateau has several deeply incised canyons in the sediments, and these are often referred to as "gulfs," which is in contrast to the use of "kill" described in the section on the Hudson-Mohawk lowlands. Rockhounding in the Tug Hill plateau is generally limited to fossils, as the rocks are almost entirely sedimentary in origin.

St. Lawrence-Champlain Lowlands

The St. Lawrence-Champlain Lowlands in New York are the lowlands along the northern and eastern sides of the Adirondacks. They are generally flat and underlain by softer early Paleozoic sandstones and carbonates. Rocks are generally only exposed in roadcuts or quarries in this province. Since most of the rocks are early Paleozoic, fossil occurrences tend to be sparse, and it takes considerable effort to find good collecting sites in many parts of this province.

Allegheny Plateau

The Allegheny Plateau is not really a plateau but a very large uplifted region that has been deeply dissected by streams and valleys. The approximate boundaries of the region are easy to make out on a state geologic map. In general, the boundaries are marked by outcrops of early Devonian sediments, and these become progressively younger in age as you enter farther west or south into the Allegheny Plateau. For the purposes of this guidebook, we are considering the Catskills region of southeastern New York, which is mainly underlain by Devonian sediments, to be part of this province. I have seen considerable debate over boundaries of the Catskills, and thought it simplest to just leave it within the Allegheny Plateau Province.

Ontario Lowlands

The Ontario Lowlands are the region along the northern end of New York that borders Lake Ontario. They are mainly underlain by Ordovician and Silurian sediments that dip slightly to the south and strike roughly east-west. This exposes the older Ordovician rocks along the shore of Lake Ontario, and the rocks become progressively younger in age as you head south towards the rocks of the Allegheny Plateau. Fossiliferous rocks are exposed along the Erie Canal between Rochester and Buffalo, and the Rochester-Ontario-Clinton area also had iron mining in the late nineteenth century.

Erie Lowlands

The Erie Lowlands are simply the low-lying areas in western New York that are adjacent to Lake Erie. They are sometimes classified with the Ontario lowlands, but the geologic rock units are much different. In contrast to the Ordovician and Silurian sedimentary rocks of the Ontario Lowlands, the rocks in the Erie Lowlands are mainly Devonian sediments. There are fossiliferous exposures on and near the coast of Lake Erie, and many areas are excellent localities for brachiopods and trilobites.

NEW YORK NATURAL RESOURCES

New York has tremendous natural resources, and these have had a profound effect on the development of the United States and the world. New York is a very large state geographically positioned to serve many large markets with its raw materials and energy. This provided the basis for its rich manufacturing heritage, which continues today. Many mines and quarries may no longer be operating, but they contributed a great deal to the economy when they were active, and in many cases literally provided the foundation for many of the roads, factories, and businesses in New York.

When collecting minerals and fossils it is often important to understand the underlying reasons for the location of mines and quarries. This will often help you identify the types of rocks you will encounter and give you some history lessons at the same time.

Iron

Iron was the first metal to be exploited in New York. The iron industry in New York dates back to the 1700s. New York iron, as well as deposits from the nearby states of Pennsylvania and New Jersey, supplied the raw material for cannon and shot for the Revolutionary War.

Iron deposits in New York included sedimentary and metamorphic deposits. The sedimentary iron ores were developed in the Silurian hematitic sediments in northwestern New York and the hematitic–limonitic ores of the Taconic Mountains. The metamorphic iron deposits were developed in the gneissic rocks of the Hudson Highlands and the Adirondacks. These deposits were very important to the local economy, but by the end of the nineteenth century, competition from the great iron ore deposits of the Mesabi Range in Minnesota made mining these deposits economically unfeasible. And by the mid- to late twentieth century, the challenging economics of natural resources doomed the great iron mines of the Adirondacks. Today all of these mines are inactive, although some attempts may be made to process the vast mine tailings of some of the large former magnetite mines into aggregate. Many of the former mine sites offer some interesting collecting opportunities, but some are on private land or state land where collecting is not allowed.

Industrial Minerals

Industrial minerals are rocks or minerals that have economic value but are not metallic ores or gemstones. Much of the successful marketing and development of industrial minerals comes from developing creative uses for these minerals and intense processing to meet customer requirements. The main industrial minerals in New York included wollastonite, garnet, and talc, which were extracted from mines in the Adirondacks. While many of New York's industrial mineral operations have closed, some key mines are still open and supplying product to their customers. These mines operate on razor-thin margins, and it is a credit to their geologists, engineers, and managers that they have been able to not just survive, but in some cases expand their domestic operations in the ultra-competitive business of industrial minerals.

Oil, Natural Gas, and Salt

Despite the current issues with a moratorium on the development of Marcellus shale wells for natural gas in New York, it is important to remember that New York, like its neighbor Pennsylvania, has a long and well-established oil and natural gas industry. As of 2013, more than 75,000 wells have been drilled in the state since the late 1800s, and about 14,000 of these wells are still active. According to the New York State Department of Environmental Conservation, Division of Mineral Resources, oil and gas development contributes nearly $500 million to New York's economy each year. From a mineral and fossil-collecting standpoint, natural gas development does not offer much in the way of new sites, but if New York ever allows development of its vast shale gas deposits, new access roads and better geologic information will be likely and may lead to some new collecting sites.

Salt could also be classified under industrial minerals, but virtually all salt mining in New York is done deep underground or by solution-mining, and it is a vastly different industry than the mining of many other nonmetallic mineral commodities. The value of the state's solution-salt-mining production alone is estimated at over $100 million. Most of the main salt mines are located in western New York. Unfortunately, from a collecting aspect, it is difficult to collect salt in New York unless you get access to an underground mine, and this is difficult for an individual collector. It is also not practical to collect outside a processing plant gate, as any salt that may have fallen out of a truck will quickly dissolve in a rain storm and wash away. Nevertheless, salt is an important mineral commodity in New York and is mentioned here for that reason.

Renewable Energy

This is an important topic, as anyone who has recently collected minerals in New York has likely seen many of the state's new huge wind farms. New York was also one of the first states to generate hydroelectric power through its power plants at Niagara Falls. However, the biggest challenge has been to get the electricity where it is generated to regions where it is needed most. This has resulted in new transmission lines and towers, many of which are fiercely opposed by environmental groups as well as landowners who do not want their property taken for a power line. From a rockhound's standpoint, new power lines may cut new exposures into mountains and provide new access roads. It is worth evaluating any new road cuts or foundations that are exposed for transmission and development.

Construction Aggregates and Cement

Construction aggregates and cement are the lifeblood of the construction industry. New York is a leader in construction aggregate and cement production as the state has vast reserves of high-quality crystalline rocks, sandstones, and limestones. While the state has a great deal of stone, environmental and permitting issues often slow the opening of new aggregate or cement rock sources, so the sites with current mining permits and high-quality reserves have often dramatically increased in value. Since the main cost associated with aggregates is transportation, the markets for stone are often local, and cement is also expensive to transport. Since the market is local, you can often see the local geology reflected in the building materials of the roads and buildings of the towns near the quarries. While quarries provide great opportunities for rock collecting, active mines often require advance permission and often can only be entered through a group or club. Abandoned quarries on state or publicly owned ground, providing they are accessible and safe, also often offer some unique opportunities to see minerals and fossils.

HOW TO USE THIS GUIDE

The sites are listed by their location in the physiographic provinces, and are generally numbered northwestward from the easternmost part of New York in Long Island to the western end of the state by Buffalo. Site names are often based on the nearest town, but in some cases I have used a local geographic feature for the locality name, especially if this will help collectors with locating the site. I have also included a New York map with the localities so you can better plan your collecting trips.

Each site entry gives GPS coordinates for parking, and if necessary, a GPS coordinate for the site itself, should you need to hike there. The coordinates are provided in the degrees, minutes, and seconds format, and are provided in the World Geodetic System (WGS 84) datum. The coordinates are rounded to the nearest second. Enter the coordinates in your GPS device, and they will take your vehicle on a route to the site. However, be aware that some GPS systems will take you on back roads and trails, and these may not be the best route to the site. In some cases, especially in rural areas, they may take you on roads and trails that may not even be made for motor vehicles.

The **finding the site** section for each site can be a good partner to your GPS as you plan your trip. In this section, a route to each site is given from the nearest major highway or, occasionally, from a nearby city. Of course, depending on where you've started, the site may be between you and that starting point, so it's a good idea to supplement your GPS and these directions with a good state highway map.

The GPS coordinates were checked against topographic maps and satellite photos. In addition, the finding the site entries were verified. I often found that the location information provided in other field guides or geologic publications was either incorrect, too vague, or purposely left out to keep collectors away. I sometimes had to visit a site multiple times before I found the right location, and even then I was sometimes unsure if I had made it to the right spot. You may use this guide and in some cases find that the spot I recommended was not as good as an adjacent location. If that happens, I apologize in advance. Be assured that I did everything that I could to accurately report what I found in the field and provide you with as much information as I could.

The site descriptions can be used to quickly provide information about a site so you will know what to expect during your visit. The **site type** refers to the type of occurrence, and this generally is a physical description of the site, which may be a streambed, roadcut, former quarry, or outcrop. The **land status** is based on the best available information and should let you know if you will be able to access the site without special permission or if you may need to secure approval from a site owner for access.

The **material** refers to the type of minerals, rocks, or fossils that a visitor would likely find of most interest. If they are listed, I can assure you that they are present at the site, but it still may take some effort to find them. In some cases if a mineral or fossil is reported to be present at a site, and I did not find it, I have listed it as "reported" if the geologic conditions are appropriate for that mineral or fossil to be present. Just because I did not find it does not mean it is not there.

The **host rock** is the rock in which the material is found, and I have generally named the geologic formation or type of rock that best describes the enclosing rocks as the host rock. It is important to understand what rocks host your materials of interest as you can use this knowledge to find similar sites.

The **difficulty** level is a guide to the likelihood of finding or observing the materials referenced in the site description. Some sites are loaded with material and you can step on to the site and find as much as you could possibly desire. Other sites take hours and hours of effort to find a single specimen, and even your most diligent efforts are not a guarantee that you will find or observe anything. If a site is marked as difficult, be aware that it may not be a good site for impatient collectors.

The **family-friendly** rating is very subjective, and depends entirely upon your family. If the description says yes without any qualifiers, you will generally find this to be a site where you can take family members who can handle moderate walking and want to look at rocks. These sites also tend to be among the easier sites to find rocks. If the description says no, generally this is because the minerals or fossils are very hard to find, or because site access is very limited or difficult.

The **tools needed** field will let you know what kind of collecting tools you should bring to a site. In most cases a rock hammer and gloves are all that are needed, but for some sites you may be best served with a chisel, flat-bladed screwdriver, large sledgehammer, or shovel. At some sites, such as beach gravels, you do not even need a hammer. I do not list standard safety equipment like boots, safety glasses, or hard hats here as the emphasis is on tools. Unfortunately, some sites, while they have interesting minerals, do not allow collecting, so in these cases this field is simply summarized as "none."

I have also included a section on **special concerns** so you know why this may not be a good site for everyone, especially if you are bringing small children. This does not mean you should not take your family, but be prepared to deal with the issues mentioned in the site description.

As mentioned previously, do not assume that this guide gives you permission to collect or to access the property. In general, all public sites in this guide can be accessed and you can look at the rocks, but many parks and government sites do not allow collecting or disturbing rocks. If the site is private, do not enter posted areas without obtaining permission, and be aware that some private ground is not often clearly posted against trespassing. In many areas ownership and the rules regarding rock collecting are not clear, so if collecting regulations are unclear at any of these sites, leave your hammer in the car and just enjoy looking at the rocks.

Map Legend

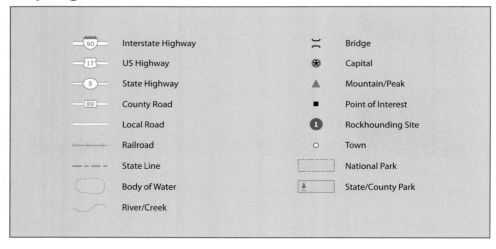

90	Interstate Highway	⌣	Bridge
17	US Highway	✪	Capital
5	State Highway	▲	Mountain/Peak
99	County Road	■	Point of Interest
	Local Road	❶	Rockhounding Site
	Railroad	○	Town
	State Line		National Park
	Body of Water		State/County Park
	River/Creek		

1. Orient Point Beach Quartz Pebbles

The pebbles are continuously reworked by the convergence of the Atlantic Ocean with Long Island Sound.

County: Suffolk
Site type: Pebbly beach
Land status: Public beach, Orient Point State Park
Material: Quartz and feldspar pebbles
Host rock: Beach gravels
Difficulty: Easy
Family-friendly: Yes
Tools needed: None
Special concerns: Collecting not allowed, near water, must be careful with small children and nonswimmers

Sites 1–3

Special attractions: Orient Point County Park
GPS parking: N41° 9' 18" / W72° 14' 27"
GPS east end of Orient Point: N41° 9' 37" / W72° 14' 00"
Topographic quadrangle: Plum Island, NY
Finding the site: This site is located near the eastern end of Long Island. From I-495, proceed east to Riverhead, and take NY 25E to Orient Point County Park. At the end of NY 25, turn right onto Dock Street, and park at the ferry parking lot. Parking is available near the ferry, and you can walk to the eastern end of Orient Point relatively easily. It is about ¾ mile from the parking area to the eastern end of the point.

Rockhounding

The beach gravels are generally rounded and range in size from pebbles to large rocks, and you can see them as soon as you reach the beach by the ferry. The white quartz is often well rounded and sometimes translucent. The white translucent quartz pebbles are similar to the quartz pebbles found at Cape May, New Jersey, which are often polished and known as Cape May diamonds. Some of the quartz pebbles have a slight orange or rose tint, and rounded pieces of granite and gneiss are also found on the

Rounded frosty quartz pebbles are abundant on the beach at Orient Point.

beach. Since this is a state park, collecting is technically not allowed, but even if you are not collecting pebbles it is still a worthwhile site to visit.

References: Eckert, 2000; Zabriskie, 2006

2. Rocky Point Beach Quartz Pebbles

The beach at Rocky Point is relatively isolated and has very nice sunsets.

(See map on page 22.)

County: Suffolk

Site type: Pebbly beach

Land status: Public beach

Material: Large white quartz pebbles

Host rock: Beach gravels

Difficulty: Easy

Family-friendly: Yes, but only if you can resolve parking issues

Tools needed: Small bag for collecting rocks, no hammer needed

Special concerns: No parking available, potentially sensitive shore property owners

Special attractions: Orient Point County Park

GPS site (no parking): N41° 08' 23" / W72° 21' 12"

Topographic quadrangle: Orient, NY

The beach has abundant round quartz pebbles.

Finding the site: This site is also located near the eastern end of Long Island. From I-495, proceed east to Riverhead, take NY 25E, and turn left (north) onto Rocky Point Road. Proceed about 1.1 miles to the intersection with Aquaview Road. The beach is reached by a stairway just north of this intersection. The main problem with this site is the lack of legal parking. It is not possible to get a temporary parking pass, and it is difficult to find any local parking. Parking by nonresidents is illegal and you run the risk of your car being ticketed or towed. A possible solution, if you have a collecting partner, is to have him drop you and your group off and return shortly afterwards.

Rockhounding

This beach has large, rounded white quartz pebbles, many of which resemble small eggs. The beach also has many large boulders of gneissic rock. It is continually reworked by the waves and the material is relatively free of sand and clay. It is not pleasant for bare feet, however, so make sure you have adequate footware. Also keep in mind that while the beach below the high-water mark may be public, the surrounding property is private. Waterfront property owners in New York pay dearly in taxes, and many are quite bitter about the high price of living adjacent to the water. Consequently they often prefer to protect their privacy and keep outsiders away. Not allowing parking is quite effective. However, as far as I could discern, the beach shoreline itself could be accessed without crossing any "no trespassing" signs.

References: Eckert, 2000

3. Lloyd Neck Cliffs Indian Paint Pots

This is half of a very large paint pot at the base of the cliffs.

(See map on page 22.)
County: Suffolk
Site type: Beach cliffs
Land status: State park, federal lands, private lands
Material: Hematite and limonite concretions, sometimes hollow
Host rock: Cretaceous sediments
Difficulty: Easy
Family-friendly: Yes
Tools needed: None
Special concerns: No collecting, no climbing on cliffs, private lands
Special attractions: Beaches and fishing at Caumsett State Park and Target Rock NWR
GPS parking, Target Rock NWR: N40° 55' 37" / W73° 26' 18"
GPS cliffs with Indian paint pots: N40° 56' 22" / W73° 28' 18"
Topographic quadrangle: Lloyd Harbor, NY

This paint pot has a hematitic shell and was filled with iron-rich sand.

Finding the site: There are two ways to access the cliffs along the northern shore of Lloyd Neck. You can park at Caumsett State Park next to their gate, and walk about 2 miles to the cliffs, as unauthorized vehicles are prohibited. I am told that if you have fishing equipment you may be able to obtain a fishing permit that will allow you to drive to the cliffs. The other option is to park at the Target Rock National Wildlife Refuge (NWR) and walk along the beach westward to the cliffs. Either way you can expect some hiking, so bring lots of water if it is summer, and dress warmly if it is cold.

The Target Rock NWR offers relatively close access to the shore if you only want to see the quartz pebbles and small pieces of hematitic conglomerates on the beach. I opted for this approach to avoid paying the state park entrance fee, but then I had to walk nearly 3 miles to the cliffs of Lloyd Neck. To get to the parking area for the Target Rock NWR, take I-495 east, and take exit 40E towards Syosset. Take NY 106 north approximately 3 miles, and turn right (east) onto NY 25. Continue about 5.5 miles, and make a slight left (north) onto Goose Hill Road. Proceed about 0.8 mile, then turn right (east) onto Huntington Road and go about 0.5 mile, where you will turn left onto West Neck Road and continue about 3.6 miles. After West Neck Road turns into Lloyd Harbor Road, continue about

2.3 miles, and turn left (north) onto Target Rock Road. In 0.3 mile, turn right onto Target Rock entrance road and proceed about 0.2 mile to the parking area on the left. There is a fee for parking.

Rockhounding

Indian paint pots are concretions of hematitic and limonitic sandstone that have hollow interiors. These formed in Cretaceous sediments in the cliffs along the north shore of Lloyd Neck. They are generally dark purple to dark red on the outside, and the interiors are sometimes full of very fine dark purple sand. They are called Indian paint pots as they were often used as paint pigments by the original inhabitants of the region. Modern artists have found that they can mix the limonite and hematite powder with linseed oil and make a distinctive and permanent yellow-brown paint.

Unfortunately, collecting and climbing the cliffs of Caumsett State Park and Target Rock NWR are prohibited. Private land is also off limits unless you have permission for access. Many schools and colleges sponsor geologic field trips to the cliffs, and the paint pots are often one of the trip highlights. Look for areas of the cliffs with brown and red staining, then look beneath these for the paint pots that have washed out of the cliffs and are now partially buried in the sand. In addition to the paint pots, the beaches have excellent rounded quartz pebbles and a wide variety of large and small loose metamorphic rocks.

If you go to these cliffs from the Target Rock NWR, be aware that while you can walk to the cliffs at low tide, the hike becomes much more difficult during high tide. In addition, during my hike to the cliffs I walked along the beach and was nearly attacked by a very large and scary looking dog. I think the owner called him "Chopper," but when I saw him all I could think of was "Cujo." When the dog charged, the owner directed me to "remain very still," which was no problem as I was already paralyzed by fear. Fortunately, this kept the dog from biting me, or perhaps it kept the dog from seeing me since I think his eyesight was very poor. On my way back, the tide came in, and I had to cross the edge of a private residence since the shoreline was now underwater and not safe to walk along. The owner was not very friendly and made it clear that they did not want people crossing the edge of their land, even for thirty seconds. Unfortunately, dealing with the occasional irate property owner is part of this hobby, especially in New York, so you must always be careful when walking near private property, especially if it is not marked as such.

References: Van Diver, 1985; Sirkin, 1996

4. Staten Island Ferry Serpentine and Gneiss

The serpentine is easy to spot as it is a dark "lizard" green.

County: Richmond
Site type: Rocks along shore
Land status: Public park
Material: Serpentine, gneiss, and granitic rocks
Host rock: All loose material, no outcrop
Difficulty: Easy
Family-friendly: Yes
Tools needed: Hammer, chisel
Special concerns: Public park, uncertain of collecting status on shoreline

Sites 4–7

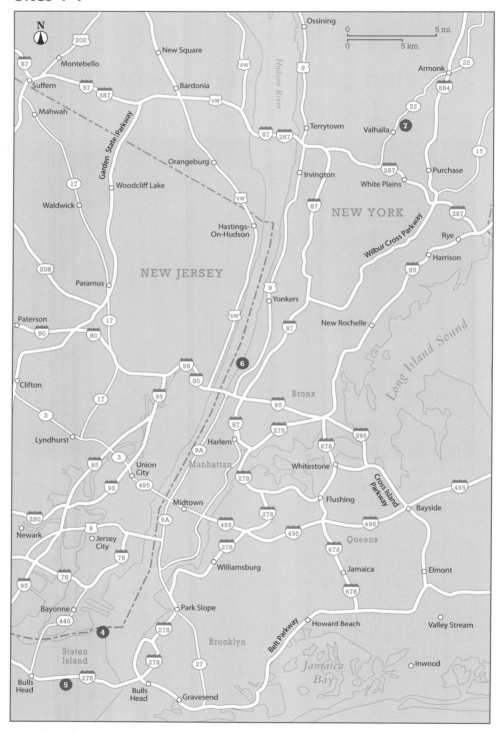

The rocks are generally well exposed west of the Staten Island Ferry, especially at low tide.

Special attractions: Staten Island Ferry, Manhattan
GPS parking: N40° 38' 47" / W74° 04' 38"
GPS rocks on shoreline: N40° 38' 50" / W74° 06' 39"
Topographic quadrangle: Jersey City, NJ
Finding the site: The Staten Island Ferry is a critical link to travel between Staten Island and lower Manhattan, and it has the huge advantage of being free and having very reasonable parking fees. When traveling to Manhattan we routinely use Staten Island as a base for parking, take the ferry, and then take the subway or walk to our destination in Manhattan. Unfortunately, getting to the Staten Island Ferry terminal in Staten Island can be a complex drive. For reference with a GPS, the Ferry is located at 1 Bay Street in Staten Island. Take I-278 to exit 13 (Clove Road/Richmond Road/Hylan Boulevard), and proceed northwest on Clove Road for approximately 0.5 mile. Turn right (northeast) onto Victory Boulevard, and continue 2.2 miles to Bay Street, then turn left (north) onto Bay Street. You will see the Staten Island Ferry on the right in about 0.3 mile. However, continue on Bay Street, which turns into Richmond Terrace, for a little over 1 mile and turn right (north) onto Jersey Street, and

then make a right onto Bank Street. Bank Street parallels the waterfront. You can easily park at the parking lot just west of Richmond County Bank Ballpark. Walk to the shoreline and you will see all of the rocks.

Rockhounding

It's very easy to find some interesting loose pieces of serpentine and garnet–bearing gneisses and schists here. The rocks were placed along Bank Road, and a walking trail runs beside it. The rocks include green banded serpentine, gar-netiferous gneisses and schists, and some of the unusual things that have fallen into the bay and floated to shore. The shoreline is loaded with driftwood as well, and watching the large container ships enter and leave the harbor is also an interesting experience. This site makes a good brief side trip before taking the ferry to New York, and is a good way to see some of the local rocks if you do not have the time to visit other localities in the New York region.

References: Beard, 2008

5. Staten Island Todt Hill Serpentine

Recent contruction activity as of 2013 has disturbed the former roadway next to the outcrops, but the outcrops are still largely intact.

(See map on page 30.)
County: Richmond
Site type: Roadcut on inactive road
Land status: Uncertain, may be a highway right-of-way
Material: Serpentine rocks and minerals
Host rock: Ordovician serpentinite
Difficulty: Easy
Family-friendly: Yes, potential good side trip when going to New York City
Tools needed: Hammer, chisel
Special concerns: Recent construction activity, access may change
Special attractions: Manhattan

Green and gray serpentine can be found throughout the roadcut.

GPS parking: N40° 36' 32" / W74° 06' 47"
GPS roadcut: N40° 36' 37" / W74° 06' 44"
Topographic quadrangle: The Narrows, NY
Finding the site: This site is easily seen from I-278 as you are crossing Staten Island, but it can be tricky to access. You cannot park on I-278 and walk to the site as there is no safe place for parking, and you do not want to get stopped by the police. It used to be possible to park on the side streets north of I-278 and cross an inactive highway bridge, but this bridge has been removed. The best way I have found to get to the roadcut is to take I-278E to exit 12 (Todt Hill Road/Slossen Avenue). This merges into Lortel Avenue. Continue to the intersection with Slossen Avenue, turn right onto Slossen Avenue, and proceed approximately 0.2 mile to Lightner Road, where you will turn left. A potential place to park is near the east end of Lightner Road near the intersection with Tillman Street. Walk to the east end of Lightner Road and follow a very indistinct trail eastward that leads to the inactive roads with the road cut. At the time of my last visit in April 2013, the land was not posted, but that is always subject to change.

Rockhounding

The road cut is an excellent exposure of Ordovician serpentine of the Manhattan Prong. The rocks are well exposed on both sides of the road, and loose serpentine can be observed along the base of the roadcuts. Much of the serpentine is light green gray, but the colors also include dark blue green. Some of the rocks have distinct banding. Most of the serpentine at this road-cut is antigorite, and associated minerals include chrysotile, hydromagnesite, artinite, and talc. Most of the serpentine I have found in this roadcut is generally massive and not fibrous, but some collectors have reportedly found some interesting specimens of chrysotile and artinite.

References: Beard, 2008

6. Inwood Park Shoreline Rocks

This is a micaceous piece of Fordham Gneiss from a large boulder next to the river.

(See map on page 30.)
County: New York
Site type: Rocks along shoreline
Land status: Inwood Park
Material: Muscovite, garnet, dravite
Host rock: Fordham Gneiss, Inwood Marble
Difficulty: Moderate
Family-friendly: No, shoreline can be tricky to hike
Tools needed: Hammer, chisel, but can only use these along shoreline rocks
Special concerns: No collecting at outcrops in the park, adjacent to Hudson River, tripping and slipping on rocks
Special attractions: The Bronx
GPS suggested parking (paid lot): N40° 52' 12" / W 73° 54' 56"
GPS shoreline area: N40° 52' 38" / W73° 55' 36"
Topographic quadrangle: Yonkers, NY

Rocks from the excavation of tunnels and other cuts were placed along the shoreline of Inwood Park, and offer the opportunity to see excavated rocks from the area.

Finding the site: The trickiest part of getting to this site is finding a suitable place to park. If you are visiting New York City you can take the subway to the Inwood Park area, but this may not be an option if you are coming from New Jersey or north of the city. I simply parked at a paid parking lot on Broadway near Isham Park. Coming from the New Jersey area, take the George Washington Bridge and take exit 1 toward New York 9A N. Once you are on New York 9A N, continue about 1.7 miles, and take exit 17 toward Dyckman Street. Merge onto Riverside Drive and take a slight left onto Broadway. Continue about 0.7 mile, then look for a paid parking area to the left. From here, walk towards Inwood Park and follow the trails and the crossing over the railroad to the Hudson River. Once you reach the picnic areas of the flat part of the park, head north along the river. The rocks are along the shoreline.

Rockhounding

Inwood Park and Isham Park are both well known for excellent exposures of Fordham Gneiss and Inwood Marble, and you will undoubtedly see many outcrops in the parks as you make your way to the Hudson River shoreline. No collecting or hammering is allowed in the parks, so stay away from the rocks in the outcrops. Instead look for the rocks that have been placed along the shoreline for bank stabilization. These have been excavated from tunnels and other excavations in the area and include large boulders of Fordham Gneiss and Inwood Marble. The gneiss often contains muscovite and garnet, and the Inwood Marble is reported to have crystals of dravite tourmaline. I was able to find some good examples of muscovite-rich gneiss, but did not find any dravite during my latest visit to the rocks. Unfortunately, unlike other sites, this area is not periodically replenished with new rocks, and erosion does not further expose more rocks. It has undoubtedly been heavily searched by previous rockhounds, so it is among the more difficult sites to find minerals, but it is a very interesting setting and well worth a visit when you are in the area.

References: Betts, 2009

7. Valhalla-Kensico Dam Quarry Orange Gneiss

The Yonkers gneiss in the quarry has patterns that suggest plastic flow when the rock was solidifying.

(See map on page 30.)
County: Westchester
Site type: Inactive quarry
Land status: Cranberry Lake Preserve
Material: Orange gneiss and pegmatites
Host rock: Granitic gneiss (Yonkers Gneiss)
Difficulty: Easy
Family-friendly: Yes
Tools needed: None
Special concerns: No collecting
Special attractions: None
GPS parking: N41° 04' 54.9" / W73° 45' 21"

Nearly all of the granitic gneiss in the quarry is a distinct orange and has a foliation that resembles tiger stripes.

GPS quarry floor: N41° 04' 21" / W73° 45' 12"
Topographic quadrangle: White Plains, NY
Finding the site: From I-87, take exit 8 towards White Plains, and merge onto I-287E. Continue 3.6 miles and take exit 6 for NY 22 towards North White Plains/White Plains. Stay on NY 22 for approximately 3.1 miles, and turn right (east) onto Old Orchard Street. Take the first right (south), and park in the parking area to the left. The trailhead to the quarry starts here. Be sure to check the map posted on the board next to the trailhead. You will want to take the loop that takes you to the quarry and not to the lake. The trail can be a little confusing but at least there is a trail to the quarry.

Rockhounding
This quarry supplied the rock for Kensico Dam. Kensico Reservoir holds much of the water supply for New York City. The dam was built in the early 1900s. The quarry is within the Cranberry Lake Preserve, which is a 190-acre park operated by the Westchester County Department of Parks. Collecting

minerals is prohibited, but it is still possible to visit the quarry and see the rocks firsthand.

The quarry is within the Yonkers Gneiss. This is a granitic gneiss that is often a distinct orange in the area of this quarry. It exhibits plastic yielding and flowage, which gives it a banded appearance, and the outcrop pattern of the gneiss often resembles tiger stripes. This is a beautiful gneiss, and I never have seen any rocks quite like this. Pegmatites with coarse white quartz and feldspar can also be found in the quarry. In addition to the white quartz and orange feldspar, the pegmatites reportedly also have large red perthitic feldspars and smoky quartz. Green microcline has also been reported from the area, but all of the feldspar that I saw was orange. During my visit to the site I was caught in an extended rainstorm, and this made it very difficult to photograph and climb on the rocks. Although collecting is not allowed, the site is still well worth a visit to see the Yonkers Gneiss and associated pegmatites. It is fortunate that the site has been preserved and is accessible to the public. If not, the area would have been developed and closed a long time ago, and we would have lost another quarry.

References: Newland, 1916; Manchester, 1931

8. Hogencamp Iron Mine

This rusty rock was nearly solid magnetite.

County: Orange
Site type: Inactive iron mine
Land status: Harriman State Park
Material: Magnetite
Host rock: Precambrian hornblende gneiss
Difficulty: Easy
Family-friendly: Yes, relatively easy hike
Tools needed: None
Special concerns: No collecting
Special attractions: Harriman State Park
GPS parking: N41° 14' 07" / W74° 07' 34"
GPS trailhead: N41° 14' 07" / W74° 07' 32"
GPS mine area: N41° 14' 40" / W74° 07' 09"

Sites 8–13

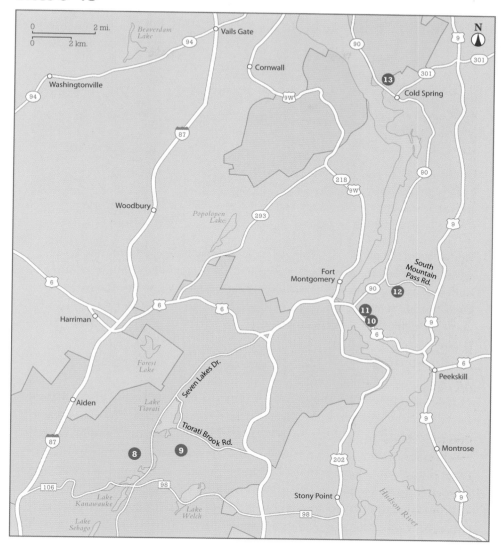

Topographic quadrangle: Thiells, NY
Finding the site: From I-87, take exit 15A to New York 17N, and proceed north. In approximately 2.5 miles, turn right (east) onto Seven Lakes Drive. Continue approximately 7 miles on Seven Lakes Drive, and you will enter a traffic circle. Take the third exit (to the west) onto CR 106W, and proceed approximately 0.9 mile to a small parking area on the right (north). The trailhead is approximately 250 feet

The remains of mining dumps serve as a reminder that this was once a very active iron mine.

to the east of the parking lot. The trail is gated and initially starts out on asphalt pavement. Follow this trail, the Dunning Trail, northeast to the mine. It has some turns and goes southeast briefly as well, but it will take you to the Hogencamp Mine in about ¾ mile. Alternatively, it is possible to access the mine through a northern trailhead of the Dunning Trail.

Rockhounding

The Hogencamp mine complex is a group of mine workings that were part of the Greenwood iron mines, which supplied iron ore to the blast furnaces at Arden, New York, until the furnaces closed around 1885. The Hogencamp mine was active from about 1870 to 1885. The Hogencamp complex is well overgrown by trees and minor underbrush, but it is still easy to identify the mine dumps, trenches, and pits. The mine dumps are rich in magnetite and have gneissic rocks with abundant biotite and hornblende. Many pieces are so rich in magnetite that they resemble pieces of steel, and they are easily spotted, as they often have a coating of orange-brown iron oxide. Some areas of the northern mine dumps also have pieces of magnetite that retain a rough octahedral crystal outline. As this is a state park, it is important to know that collecting is not allowed, but it still is well worth visiting to observe the abundant magnetite and associated minerals.

References: Clark, 1921; Gates, 2003; Lenik, 1999; Reis, 1895

9. Hasenclever Iron Mine

The ore at the Hasenclever mine was fine-grained magnetite.

(See map on page 43.)
County: Rockland
Site type: Former Iron Mine
Land status: Harriman State Park
Material: Magnetite
Host rock: Gneiss and schist
Difficulty: Easy
Family-friendly: Yes
Tools needed: None
Special concerns: No collecting, flooded mine pit, state park
Special attractions: Harriman State Park
GPS parking: N41° 15' 30.1"/ W74° 04' 49.7"
GPS mine site: N41° 15' 04.6"/ W74° 04' 59.2"
Topographic quadrangle: Popolopen Lake, NY
Finding the site: This parking area for this site is in Orange County, but the mine itself is in Rockland County. From I-87, take exit 15A to New York Highway 17N,

The mine dumps of the Hasenclever mine are right next to the trail.

and proceed north. In approximately 2.5 miles, turn right (east) onto Seven Lakes Drive. Continue approximately 10.2 miles on Seven Lakes Drive, and you will enter a traffic circle (there are other traffic circles on the way). Take the first exit onto Tiorati Brook Road, and proceed 1.7 miles to the small parking area on the left (north) side of the road. The trailhead is approximately 200 feet west of the parking area. Follow the trail, which is the "red cross" trail, south approximately half a mile to the Hasenclever mine, which is easy to spot as it has a water-filled pit and several mine dumps in the woods next to the pit.

Rockhounding

This is one of the oldest of the iron mines in the Hudson Highlands. The Hasenclever mine was discovered and developed in 1765 by Peter Hasenclever, who was an early iron entrepreneur in the region. During the Revolutionary War the mine was worked by Samuel Brewster, and it was purchased by Jonas Brewster in 1799. A blast furnace was built near the mine around 1800. The mine was worked for much of the nineteenth century by various other operators, and its final year was in 1891, during which it was worked by A. Lawrence Edmonds, who was an associate of Thomas Edison.

The dumps near the water-filled pit are full of gneisses with fine-grained disseminated magnetite, and the rocks are generally amphibolites, schists, and minor zones of granitic pegmatite. It is easy to identify the most iron-rich rocks, as these often have an orange-brown tint and are extremely dense. The dumps are just west of the water-filled pit and extend into the woods.

References: Lenik, 1996

10. Bear Mountain Highway 6 Minerals

This gneissic rock with epidote was found along the hillside downslope of the parking area.

(See map on page 43.)
County: Westchester
Site type: Hillside with rocks dumped from roadcuts
Land status: Uncertain, not posted
Material: Epidote, garnet
Host rock: Canada Hill Granite and Grenville Gneiss
Difficulty: Moderate to difficult
Family-friendly: No, slope is very steep and covered with trash
Tools needed: Hammer, chisel, small backpack to carry out rocks
Special concerns: Steep slope, lots of trash on hillside
Special attractions: Scenic parking area view
GPS parking: N41° 18' 42" / W73° 58' 14"
Topographic quadrangle: Peekskill, NY

The land downslope of the parking area is extremely steep and full of trash as well as rocks.

Finding the site: From I-87N, take exit 16 and follow the signs towards NY 17 toward US 6E. This is a tricky set of intersections but your goal is to get on US 6E. Continue approximately 9.6 miles east to the Bear Mountain Bridge. You will pass two large traffic circles on the way. Cross Bear Mountain Bridge, turn right (south) and continue 0.7 mile on US 6, which is also US 202 and known as the Bear Mountain Parkway. You will then see a large parking area where the road turns to the east. There is space for several cars to park, and the lot generally has at least one or two cars at any time stopping for pictures along the Hudson River. The rocks are not at the roadcut, but are downslope and east of the parking area. Do not try to access the roadcut, as the area on the mountain side of the highway is extremely dangerous.

Rockhounding

The target rocks here are those pushed over the embankment when US 6 was widened in March 1991. I have been at this site twice, and focused on the rocks downslope of the parking area. The embankment is extremely steep and full of trash dumped from the parking area. Make certain that you have good gloves and boots. Do not attempt this site with sandals, shorts, or other clothing, which will not protect you from the glass, trash, unstable rocks, and poison ivy. I was able to find some epidote and garnet, but overall was not impressed with the material that I was finding downslope, especially for the price that I paid in climbing down a steep, unstable slope full of trash and poison plants. Later, when rereading some of the references for the site, I found that the

This outcrop is at the southeast corner of the Bear Mountain Bridge, and while not part of this site, it may be representative of some of the rocks blasted from the roadcut.

best material was reportedly about 50 yards east of the parking area, and not immediately downslope. Unfortunately I have not yet been back to the site, but certainly intend to give it another shot when I am back in the area. This site has the significant advantage of having a large parking area and it is very close to the rocks, although the rocks are not in the easiest place to reach. It is likely another example of a site that I have to visit multiple times before I find the right spot. If you go to this site, I definitely recommend checking out the areas east of the parking area instead of immediately downslope.

Nearby I also found an example that may be representative of the rocks blasted from the roadcut. There is an outcrop on the east end of the Bear Mountain Bridge, just north of this area, only 0.7 mile from this site. To get there, turn left (north) onto NY 9D after crossing Bear Mountain Bridge. You will be on the Bear Mountain-Beacon Highway. There is a parking area along the west side of the highway for hikers. Continue north until you can make a U-turn, and come back and park at the parking area. Now walk to the south-east corner of the bridge, being extremely careful of the traffic, and check out the rocks next to the road behind the stone wall. They are gneissic rocks loaded with brown garnet, light-green epidote, and tiny blebs of what appears to be graphite. Although this is not part of this site, it is worth mentioning, as it is certainly one of the best mineralized outcrops in the area.

References: Betts, 1997; Zabriskie, 2006

11. Hudson Railroad Cut Calcite

The east bank of the Hudson River is lined with boulders of gneiss, schist, and carbonate, and the calcite crystals are found in the tan carbonate boulders.

(See map on page 43.)

County: Westchester

Site type: Boulders and large rocks along river bank

Land status: Uncertain, not posted

Material: Calcite crystals

Host rock: Tan carbonate rocks

Difficulty: Moderate

Family-friendly: No, train tunnel can be dangerous for large groups of people

Tools needed: Hammer, chisel

Special concerns: Trains

Special attractions: None

GPS parking: N41° 19' 14" / W73° 58' 41"

GPS calcite crystals: N41° 18' 53" / W73° 58' 35"

Topographic quadrangle: Peekskill, NY

Finding the site: From I-87N, take exit 16 and follow the signs towards New York 17 toward US 6E. This is a tricky set of intersections but your goal is to get on US 6E. Continue approximately 9.6 miles east to the Bear Mountain Bridge. You will pass two large traffic circles on the way. Cross Bear Mountain Bridge, and turn left (north) onto NY 9D, which is the Bear Mountain-Beacon Highway. You will see a parking area along the west side of the highway for hikers in the area. Continue north until you can make a U-turn, and come back and park at the parking area. From here, go to the north side of the Bear Mountain Bridge, and look for a trail that descends along the bridge wall towards the Hudson River. This has some switchbacks but it eventually takes you to the railroad tracks. From here, walk south along the tracks. You can walk through the tunnels but you must walk through very rapidly, and make sure that there are no approaching trains. The trains are numerous and very quiet until they pass you, and then they are extremely noisy. Follow the tracks south and look for calcite and other minerals in the boulders along the riverbank just west of the railroad tracks.

The piece with calcite crystals was broken off a boulder next to the river bank.

Rockhounding

This is a difficult site to reach due to the hiking, the tunnels, and the trains, but can be worth the trip. The calcite is found in tan carbonate rocks along the shore of the Hudson River. These rocks were reportedly from the excavation of the railroad tunnels. The rocks near the tunnels have been sprayed with gunnite and partially covered with tar, and I did not see any good rocks next to the tunnels. There is a wide variety of rocks along the shore of the Hudson River, and most of these rocks are large boulders that were placed for bank stabilization. These include gneisses and schists as well as the carbonates. While some of the gneisses and schists have some interesting occurrences of hornblende and garnet, the best crystals that I found along the river were the calcite in the carbonate rocks, and the best crystals appeared to be in the tan, vuggy boulders and large rocks. You will have to break them open to expose the best sections with crystals. As mentioned previously, you have to be very careful of the trains at this site, and be ready for a fairly strenuous hike down to the river and adjacent tracks.

References: Betts, 1997

12. Philips Mine Sulfides

The Philips Mine was first worked in the early 1800s for iron, and has also been worked for sulfur and copper.

(See map on page 43.)

County: Putnam

Site type: Former mine and mine dumps

Land status: Palisades Interstate Park

Material: Pyrite, pyrrhotite, hornblende, magnetite

Host rock: Quartz diorite, pyroxene diorite, monzonite

Difficulty: Easy

Family-friendly: Yes

Tools needed: Hammer, chisel

Special concerns: Trail to mine is indistinct, some climbing/bushwacking needed

Special attractions: Appalachian Trail

GPS parking: N41° 19' 47" / W73° 57' 09"

GPS mine site: N41° 19' 38" / W73° 57' 08"

Topographic quadrangle: Peekskill, NY

Finding the site: From I-87, as you approach Harriman, take NY 17W, proceed to the intersection with NY 32, turn south onto NY 17, and then onto US 6E. Cross the Hudson River via the Bear Mountain Bridge. Immediately after you cross the bridge, turn left (north) onto NY 9D. Proceed 1.3 miles, and make a slight turn to the right onto Manitou Road. Proceed 0.2 mile, then turn east onto South Mountain Pass Road. Continue 0.5 mile to the parking area, which will be on the right. It is likely that other cars will be parked here to access the Appalachian Trail. Proceed to the gate on the trail, and hike southward into the woods. The Philips Mine is approximately 1,000 feet south of the gate. Look for an open area in the trees, and also watch for changes in the soil as you approach the mine. You will likely see some orange/brown rocks that washed downgradient from the mine dumps.

Large masses of hornblende with sulfides are common on the mine dumps.

Rockhounding

Metallic sulfide mines are very difficult to reclaim, and they are generally easy to find, as very few plants will grow on the former workings. The Philips Mine is certainly no exception. The mine was originally started as an iron mine around 1835, but the high sulfur content from the pyrrhotite and pyrite undoubtedly made the ores much less attractive than those from other nearby iron mines. After the Civil War the mine was worked for copper, and near the end of the nineteenth century was worked for sulfur to produce sulfuric acid. Mining and smelting sulfides for sulfur is pretty messy, and the environmental issues with air and water quality must have been horrific. However, the mine was also reportedly free of arsenic, and this made the ores much more valuable. In 1907 the mine was again reopened as a copper mine. After World War II the mine was explored for uranium minerals, but the uranium mineralization was marginal and the deposits were never developed.

At the present time the Philips mine is an interesting site for rockhounds and scientists studying the effects of metallic sulfide mining in a New York watershed. It is located on parklands just north of the Appalachian Trail. The dumps have abundant pyrite, pyrrhotite, and hornblende, and apatite and epidote are also reported at the mine site. It is very easy to find large hand samples of dense rock that is loaded with pyrite and other sulfides, and the hornblende gives many of the rocks a unique bladed character.

References: Betts, 1997; Heyl, 1997; Klemic et al. 1959

13. Mount Taurus Quarry

This gneiss has coarse white to tan feldspar and black hornblende.

(See map on page 43.)
County: Putnam
Site type: Inactive quarry
Land status: Hudson Highlands State Park
Material: Amphiboles and associated minerals
Host rock: Gneiss
Difficulty: Easy
Family-friendly: Yes
Tools needed: None
Special concerns: No collecting, state park, cliff sides steep, rocks unstable
Special attractions: Hudson Highlands State Park
GPS parking: N41° 25' 36" / W73° 57' 35"
GPS quarry: N41° 25' 43" / W73° 57' 43"
Topographic quadrangle: West Point, NY

Finding the site: From I-84, take exit 11 for NY 9D toward Beacon/Wappinger Falls. Continue south on NY 9D for approximately 7.7 miles, and look for the parking area, which is on the east side of NY 9D S and directly opposite the entrance to Little Stony Point. Park here, walk to the north end of the parking area, and follow the Cornish Trail to the quarry. The hike is fairly steep and it is hard to believe that you are going to a quarry, but in about ½ mile you will come to a very broad flat area that is the floor of the former Mount Taurus quarry.

The sides of the quarry are covered with loose gneissic rocks.

Rockhounding

This site is an abandoned, inactive quarry, and it is also referred to as the Bull Hill Quarry. It was opened in 1931 by the Hudson River Stone Corporation. Stone was quarried and conveyed down the hill and loaded onto barges. The operation closed in 1967, and the area became part of Hudson Highlands State Park in 1970. The rocks are a hard gneiss, and much of the gneiss is strongly foliated and shows excellent banding. Some of the coarsely crystalline rocks have large black amphiboles in white-to-tan gneissic rock. This is a unique opportunity to look at a former quarry and explore broken rocks that are still relatively freshly exposed, even though the quarry has been inactive since 1967.

References: Adams, 1996

14. Amity-Pine Island Calcite

This marble outcrop is along the north side of Walling Road.

County: Orange
Site type: Roadcuts
Land status: Private, must stay within road right-of-ways
Material: Calcite with graphite
Host rock: Franklin Marble
Difficulty: Easy
Family-friendly: No, limited outcrops, specialty mineral collecting
Tools needed: Hammer, chisel
Special concerns: Private property, traffic along roads
Special attractions: "Black dirt" of local farmlands
GPS Parking-Walling Road: N41° 16' 17" / W74° 28' 01"
GPS Parking-Prices Switch Road: N41° 15' 21" / W74° 27' 17"
GPS Parking-Horseshoe Lane: N41° 16' 59" / W74° 25' 50"
Topographic quadrangle: Pine Island, NY
Finding the site: This is a site where you really have to have a local street map, as the collecting is all along roadcuts. I highly recommend printing a map from

Site 14

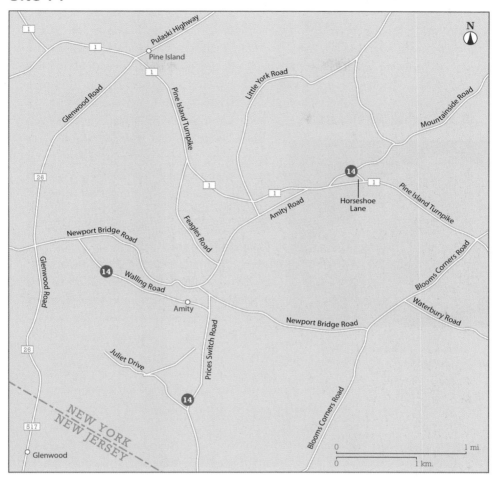

Google, Mapquest, or any other reliable Internet map provider. Since Pine Island is a slightly larger town, I recommend starting in Pine Island and driving to the local roadcuts. To get to Pine Island from I-87, take exit 16 for NY 17W. Once on 17W, proceed about 9 miles to exit 126 for NY 94. Take NY 94W for 4.3 miles through the town of Florida, where it becomes Meadow Road. Continue another 0.5 mile, and Meadow will turn into CR 25, Pumpkin Swamp Road. Continue 1.5 miles, then turn left onto CR 6/Pulaski Highway, and continue 5.2 miles to Pine Island. From here you can use your local map and GPS to go to the various roadcuts around Amity and south of Pine Island.

Rockhounding

I have originally stayed away from this area, as the entire region is private land and I was uncertain of its collecting/access status. However, an excellent website operated by Jeff Wilson, an experienced local collector in the region, indicated that collecting could be possible on the roadcuts of the area. Jeff mentioned several roads on his site, and I was able to visit outcrops along Walling Road, Prices Switch Road, and Horseshoe Lane. The cuts on Walling Road and Horseshoe Lane have outcrops of marble, and the cut along

This piece of calcite with graphite blebs was found in the wash along Prices Switch Road.

Prices Switch Road is more like a wash with calcite pieces in the soil. The rocks that I found were limited to white-to-tan calcite with blebs of graphite, but diopside, franklinite, spinel, hornblende, phlogopite, and many other minerals are reported to be available. Some of the rocks reportedly are fluorescent, and this is not surprising, as they are located just northeast of the world-famous minerals of the Franklin, New Jersey, region. Jeff recommended visiting the Amity area in early spring after the snowplows rip up the roadside, and given the narrow roads, this is an excellent idea. Parking is very limited in the area, and all of the area is private land, so be sure to stay out of areas that are posted against trespassing. It is best to limit collecting to loose rocks that you find on the roadside or outcrops that are clearly in the road right-of-way. Most of the properties near the road also have extensive rock walls, and while many of these are mineralized, do not collect or otherwise disturb these walls.

Another interesting aspect of this area is that it is known as "Black Dirt" country. This was dark, fertile soil from a glacial lake bottom and flooding of the Wallkill River. The "Black Dirt" covers nearly 26,000 acres and is reportedly the largest concentration of such soil in the United States outside of the Florida Everglades. As you drive around looking for roadcuts, especially when you come to valley overlooks, you will get some excellent views of the huge fields of black soil, and they are quite impressive.

References: Kearns, 1978; Manchester, 1931; Gordon, 1990

15. Millerton Iron Mine Pond Blue Slag

Iron Mine Pond is the site of a former iron mine.

County: Dutchess
Site type: Former mine and furnace
Land status: Taconic State Forest
Material: Limonite and glassy blue slag
Host rock: Weathered Precambrian schist
Difficulty: Easy
Family-friendly: Yes
Tools needed: None
Special concerns: No collecting, mosquitoes
Special attractions: Copake Iron Furnace
GPS parking: N41° 58' 03" / W73° 29' 51"
GPS dam site with slag: N41° 58' 08" / W73° 29' 52"

Sites 15–16

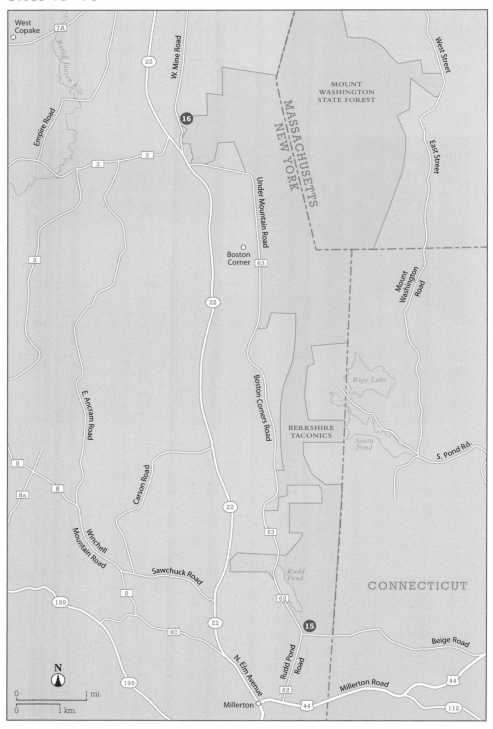

West Copake

7A

22

W. Mine Road

16

MASSACHUSETTS
NEW YORK

MOUNT
WASHINGTON
STATE FOREST

West Street

East Street

Empire Road

Roeliff Jansen Kill

3

3

3

Under Mountain Road

Boston
Corner

63

Mount
Washington
Road

22

Riga Lake

E. Ancram Road

Boston Corners Road

BERKSHIRE
TACONICS

South
Pond

S. Pond Rd.

8

8a

8

Carson Road

22

63

Winchell
Mountain Road

Sawchuck Road

8

22

199

60

N. Elm Avenue

Rudd
Pond

Rudd Pond
Road

62

15

CONNECTICUT

Beige Road

199

N

Millerton

62

44

Millerton Road

44

112

0   1 mi.

0   1 km.

Topographic quadrangle: Sharon, CT
Finding the site: From the Taconic State Parkway, take the exit for NY 199, and proceed about 12.6 miles to the intersection with CR60/Winchell Mountain Road. Proceed about 2.3 miles, and take a slight right onto NY 22S. Go about 0.6 mile, turn left (east) onto Main Street, and take the second left (north) onto Rudd Pond Road. Follow this about 1 mile to the intersection with Shagroy Road, where you will turn right (east). The parking area is on the left (north) side of the road.

Glassy blue slag can be found around the dam and in the stream that exits the pond.

Rockhounding

Iron Mine Pond was the site of the Maltby Iron Mine. A furnace was built at the mine site around 1847, and the mine was purchased by Caleb A. Maltby in 1861. The mine produced a high grade of iron for railroad-car wheels. Unfortunately, the mine ultimately could not compete with the ores produced in the great iron ranges of Minnesota, and the mine closed for good by 1893. The mine pit soon filled with water and became known as Iron Mine Pond.

Today the area is within the Taconic State Forest. Although collecting is not allowed, it is possible to hike around the pond. A small waterfall over weathered schist is on the northeast side of the pond, and small fragments of the original ore, which was a yellow-brown limonite, can still be found in the hillside and along the shoreline near the waterfall. A dam site near the southwest side of the pond has abundant glassy blue slag and much more limonite, and this apparently was near the site of a former iron furnace. The creek adjacent to the parking area also has a lot of blue and light purple slag, and these can easily be spotted in the bottom of the stream from the banks. This area is a good place to show kids slag, as the creek is very small and close to the parking area, and the slag is quite colorful.

References: Budnik et al., 2010; Eckert, 2000

16. Weed Mines
Limonite and Hematite

The ores were mainly limonite and hematite, and iron-bearing rocks are common on the shoreline.

(See map on page 60.)
County: Columbia
Site type: Loose rocks on shoreline
Land status: Taconic State Forest
Material: Limonite and hematite
Host rock: Weathered schist
Difficulty: Moderate
Family-friendly: No, very limited access to shoreline
Tools needed: None
Special concerns: No collecting, steep shoreline, mosquitoes
Special attractions: Fishing in Weed Mines Pond, Copake Iron Works
GPS parking: N42° 04' 38" / W73° 32' 06"
GPS shoreline with limonite and hematite: N42° 04' 32" / W73° 31' 54"
Topographic quadrangle: Copake, NY

Weed Mines Pond was formed by a long narrow iron mine.

Finding the site: From the Taconic State Parkway, take NY 23E, and continue about 7.1 miles to the intersection with NY 22S. Turn right (south) on NY 22S, and proceed about 8.1 miles. Turn left (east) onto a sharp turn that leads to Weed Mines Road, which then goes north. The parking area, which is marked by a small sign, is on the left (east) side of the road. Park here, and walk south on the trail. Approximately ⅛ mile farther on the trail will be a small, indistinct footpath to the left (east). Follow this to the steep shoreline of Weed Mines Pond.

Rockhounding

The Weed Mines are one of several limonite-hematite iron deposits that were mined during the last part of the nineteenth century. This is one of the few sites with public access where you can see some of the remaining mineralization. The site is in Taconic State Park, so collecting is not allowed, but you can still easily see some of the limonite and hematite along the shoreline of Weed Mines Pond. The limonite/hematite rocks are very heavy when compared to the nonmineralized rocks, and large rocks that are intergrown with tree roots are alongside the lake. These are easily recognized, as they are red and light brown. The exteriors resemble conglomerates, as they are composed of many individual rock fragments, and the interiors generally exhibit weak banding and layering of alternating bands of various shades of limonite and hematite.

References: Newland, 1919

17. South Bay Roadside Quarry Ripple Marks

These ripple marks were found in a loose piece on the quarry floor.

County: Washington
Site type: Roadside quarry
Land status: Active roadside quarry, not posted
Material: Ripple marks and banded sandstone
Host rock: Cambrian Potsdam Sandstone
Difficulty: Easy
Family-friendly: No, lots of loose rocks, land status questionable
Tools needed: Hammer, chisel
Special concerns: Quarry active at times
Special attractions: Lake George
GPS parking: N43° 33' 55" / W73° 28' 22.8"
Topographic quadrangle: Whitehall, NY
Finding the site: From I-87, take exit 20, Fort Ann/Whitehall, towards NY 149. Turn left onto CR 23, proceed 0.2 mile, then turn left onto NY 149/US 9N, and proceed about 0.7 mile. Turn right onto NY 149E, and continue 11.7 miles to US 4 N/George

Sites 17–18

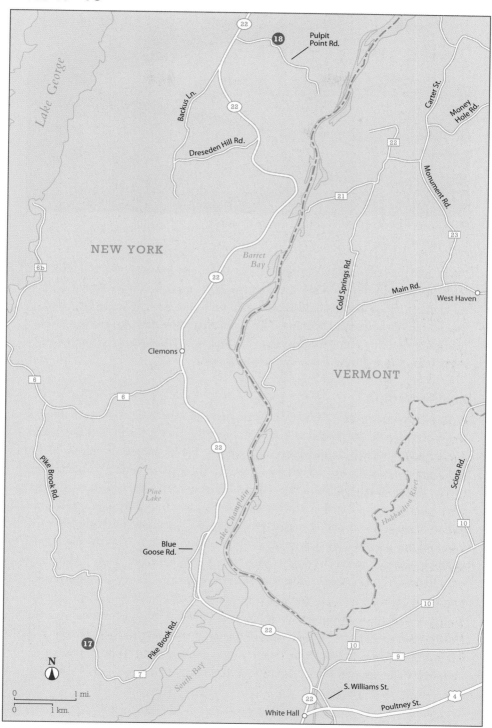

Lake George

22 **18** Pulpit Point Rd.

Backus Ln.

Carter St.

Money Hole Rd.

22

Dreseden Hill Rd.

22

21

23

NEW YORK

Barret Bay

Cold Springs Rd.

Main Rd.

West Haven

6b

22

6

Clemons

VERMONT

6

6

22

Sciota Rd.

Pike Brook Rd.

Pine Lake

10

Lake Champlain

Hubbardton River

Blue Goose Rd.

10

17

Pike Brook Rd.

10

22

10

9

N

7

South Bay

S. Williams St.

4

22

Poultney St.

0   1 mi.

0   1 km.

White Hall

The quarry is adjacent to Pike Brook Road and is easy to find.

Street, and turn left (north). Continue 10.6 miles to the fork with NY 22/Broadway Street, and follow US 22N (veer left, or north, at the fork). Continue 3 miles, and turn left onto Blue Goose Road. Continue 0.1 mile, then turn left onto CR 7, and proceed 3 miles. This road becomes Pike Brook Road. The parking area will be on the right (east) side of the road, and the quarry is easily visible on the left (west) side of the road. Plenty of parking space is available.

Rockhounding

I visited the quarry on a Sunday in April 2013, and the quarry was not active at the time and was not posted. It is adjacent to Pike Brook Road, and the eastern side may extend into the roadside right-of-way. The quarry is apparently part of the mining operations of Champlain Stone, Ltd., which operates a much larger quarry to the north and has some other stone extraction operations to the west. The quarry is unique in that most of the surrounding mountains are igneous and metamorphic rocks, and this quarry is in sandstone. The sandstone is generally fine grained and has attractive banding, but the most unique feature is the abundance of ripple marks. Some of the ripple marks are quite large, but many loose pieces with distinct ripple marks can be found throughout the quarry. If you go to this site, do not enter if it is active, and do not enter if it becomes posted or otherwise inaccessible. If you are not comfortable with entering the quarry area, you may also be able to see some ripple marks in the rocks on the side of the road.

References: Penn, 2009

18. Pulpit Point Road Graphite Boulders

Shiny black graphite is common on the boulders at this site.

(See map on page 65.)
County: Washington
Site type: Mineralized boulders with graphite
Land status: Uncertain, not posted in area of the boulders
Material: Graphite
Host rock: Pegmatite, coarse granitic rocks
Difficulty: Easy
Family-friendly: No, limited space, boulder climbing
Tools needed: Hammer, chisel
Special concerns: Limited parking, land not posted but likely private
Special attractions: Lake George
GPS parking: N43° 42' 42" / W73° 25' 06"

The boulders are easy to spot on the north side of Pulpit Point Road.

Topographic quadrangle: Putnam, NY

Finding the site: From I-87, take exit 28 for NY 7E towards Ticonderoga. Continue 18.9 miles to Ticonderoga, and turn left (south) onto NY 22S. Proceed 10.5 miles, and turn left onto Pulpit Point Road. Continue 0.6 mile, where you will see the boulders on the north side of the road. While the surrounding areas are posted as private land, the area of the boulders is not posted, and it is very close to the road. Parking is very limited, and the best place for a vehicle is on the south side of the road approximately 200 feet north of the boulder location.

Rockhounding

The boulders on the north side of Pulpit Point Road are reportedly from a graphite mine that was located nearby. However, the mine is not marked on the topographic quadrangle for the area, and it is not obviously visible on any recent or historical aerial photographs. The boulders, which are on the north side of the road and easy to locate as you are driving along Pulpit Point Road, are generally highly mineralized and have an abundance of soft, shiny black graphite. Apatite and rose quartz are also reported to occur on the boulders. Although the land is not posted, it is in an area that is surrounded by private land, so be aware that access to this site is subject to change.

References: Zabriskie, 2006

19. Highland Mills Fossils

The fossils are best found by breaking open the rocks.

County: Orange
Site type: Railroad cut
Land status: Private, not posted
Material: Brachiopods
Host rock: Devonian Esopus Formation
Difficulty: Easy
Family-friendly: No, due to train tracks
Tools needed: None
Special concerns: Train traffic
Special attractions: Bear Mountain and Harriman State Parks
GPS parking: N41° 20' 40" / W74° 07' 14"
GPS outcrop: N41° 20' 42" / W74° 07' 12"

Sites 19–21

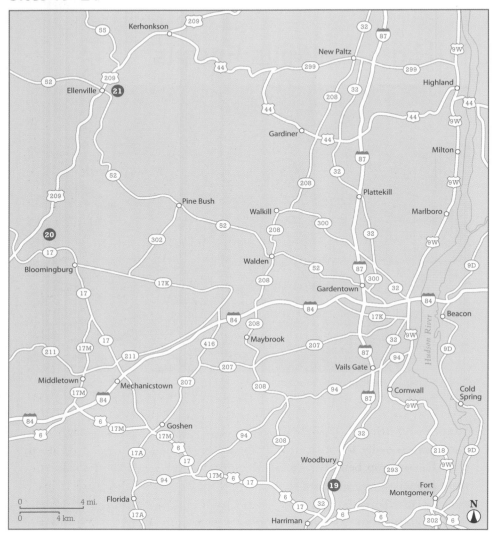

Topographic quadrangle: Popolopen Lake, NY
Finding the site: From I-87, take exit 16 for NY 17W towards US 6/Harriman. Turn right (north) on NY 32, and proceed 2.3 miles to Park Avenue. Turn right (east), and proceed 0.3 mile to a small gravel parking area. Park here, walk towards the railroad tracks, and you will see the fossil-bearing outcrop on the east side of the tracks.

Trains are frequent at this site and you must stay well away from them.

Rockhounding

This site has steeply dipping rocks of the Middle Devonian Esopus Formation, which consists of fine-grained sandstone with interbedded shale. The beds dip about 65° northwest. The fossils occur as brachiopod shell "hash" layers, and they are generally found as iron-stained molds. As you walk farther north from this outcrop, being extremely careful to stay off the tracks, the sediments are younger, more shale rich, and less fossiliferous, so your fossil collecting is best at this outcrop. I also headed slightly south of this outcrop, but still found the best fossils were at this location. Close inspection of the outcrop revealed that the fossils are confined to only a few beds in a relatively narrow section of these sediments. While the fossils are not in abundance, they are generally well formed, and the rocks have some attractive iron staining. Some interesting trace fossils can also be found at this site.

References: US Geological Survey, 2003

20. Wurtsboro Lead Mines

The dumps of the upper workings are extensive, and mining in the region began around 1830. The area is now restricted to access due to the discovery of lead contamination in 2012.

(See map on page 70.)
County: Sullivan
Site type: Former lead mines
Land status: Wurtsboro Ridge Open Space, reportedly public access
Material: Galena, sphalerite, pyrite, quartz
Host rock: Mineralized Silurian Shawangunk conglomerate
Difficulty: Easy, except for hiking to upper workings
Family-friendly: No, due to potential for lead contamination
Tools needed: Hammer, chisel
Special concerns: Site recently closed to entry by state regulators
Special attractions: Shawangunk Mountains
GPS parking for upper lead mine: N41° 34' 37" / W74° 27' 53"
GPS upper lead mine: N41° 35' 37" / W74° 26' 39"
GPS parking for lower lead mine: N41° 35' 19" / W74° 27' 38"

The lower workings have staining near the dumps due to mine drainage that has leached many of the metals from the rocks.

GPS lower lead mine: N41° 35' 43" / W74° 27' 03"
Topographic quadrangle: Wurtsboro, NY
Finding the site: To reach the upper lead mine, take US 209N into Wurtsboro. Turn right (southeast) onto Sullivan Street, go 0.8 mile, and stay to the left on Mamakating Road. Go 0.5 mile, and turn left (northeast) onto V F W Road. Go 0.2 mile to the end of the road and park. From here, hike northeast on an old road, and when you cross a small stream that goes under the dirt road, take the trail that goes up the mountain. This trail leads to the mine. The road hike is easy, but the trail up the mountain is very strenuous. The mine is nearly 2 miles from the parking area, so bring plenty of water, especially during the summertime. I highly recommend using your GPS and satellite photos before you come to this site, as it can be tricky to find, especially if you take the wrong trail.

To reach the lower lead mine, go back to Wurtsboro via Sullivan Street. Turn right (northeast) on US 209N. Go 1.2 miles, and turn right (southeast) onto McDonald Road. Follow this road to a small creek, and you will see an area where cars can park. From here, hike along the path that parallels the Delaware and Hudson Canal. Approximately 4,000 feet later you will see a small path that heads southeast, and looking through the trees you will be able to see a white mine dump. These are the lower workings. Again, I recommend using your GPS and an air photo to make sure that you do not walk by the workings.

Rockhounding

Unfortunately, the State of New York recently closed both the upper and lower workings access by putting up a sign warning of lead contamination and stating no one is permitted to enter. Despite the fact that the mines have been there since 1830, the contamination was "discovered" by the New York State Department of Environmental Conservation in 2012. There was no fencing around the site, and I saw indications that people still visit the area. As of April 2013 I saw no evidence that the state has proceeded with any remediation or further work other than putting up signs. Since this has historically been an important local site for rockhounds, it has been kept in this guide so visitors can still find the mines and know what to expect.

The Shawangunk lead mines are among the oldest mines in the United States. They were worked extensively from 1830 to 1840, and high-grade lead ore was extracted, but the mines were then idle except for a brief period during World War I. The mines were studied again by the US Geological Survey and the US Bureau of Mines in the late 1940s. The upper mines are reached via a fairly strenuous hike, and the dumps are a prominent feature of the hillside. Not surprisingly, nothing grows on the dumps so they are easy to spot. There is also reportedly another mine upslope of this mine, and it is visible in satellite photographs of the area. The lower mines are much easier to reach, but unfortunately have the same sign stating no one is permitted to enter.

The minerals at these workings are reported to be mainly galena, quartz, and pyrite. Sphalerite is also reported at both workings. While collectors have been coming to this site for decades, the closure by the state will likely be in place for the foreseeable future. We will continue to see similar sites closed over time. Like all former mine sites, enter the property at your own risk. If you decide to go to these sites, avoid getting mineral dust on your bare skin and clothes, and do not lick your fingers or eat your lunch on a rock with crusts of lead-bearing mud.

References: Sims and Hotz, 1951; Zabriskie, 2006; Mayer, 2012

21. Ellenville Pyrite and Quartz

Disseminated pyrite is common to the quarry, especially near the southwestern corner.

(See map on page 70.)
County: Ulster
Site type: Former quarry
Land status: Local parkland
Material: Pyrite and quartz
Host rock: Mineralized Silurian Shawangunk conglomerate
Difficulty: Easy
Family-friendly: Yes
Tools needed: Hammer, chisel
Special concerns: None
Special attractions: Shawangunk Mountains
GPS parking: N41° 42' 48" / W74° 22' 57"
GPS quarry: N41° 42' 43" / W74° 22' 55"
Topographic quadrangle: Ellenville, NY
Finding the site: From US 209N, enter Ellenville, and turn right (southeast) onto Center Street, and go 0.6 mile. Turn left (northeast) onto Broadhead Street, go 0.1

The quarry is just up the hill from the parking area.

mile, and continue onto Berme Road. You will then be entering a park area. Park here, and follow the trail up the hill to the quarry.

Rockhounding

This site is easy to reach and has some interesting massive pyrite and small quartz crystals. The quarry is frequently visited by park users, and lots of loose rock with pyrite and quartz crystals can be found throughout much of the quarry. The most mineralized zones that I saw were near the southwestern corner of the quarry. Much of the most mineralized rock is on smooth surfaces and difficult to break off, so in many cases it is best to leave these zones for the next visitors to enjoy.

References: Eckert, 2000; Hawkins, 2007

22. Kingston Highway 32 Calcite Crystals

This aggregate of calcite crystals would require a hammer and chisel to remove, and it would take some signifcant effort.

County: Ulster
Site type: Roadcuts
Land status: Uncertain, not posted
Material: Calcite crystals
Host rock: Early Devonian Manlius Limestone
Difficulty: Moderate
Family-friendly: No, limited material, traffic and parking issues
Tools needed: Hammer, chisel
Special concerns: Very limited parking
Special attractions: None
GPS parking: N41° 58' 10" / W73° 58' 17"
Topographic quadrangle: Kingston East, NY

Sites 22–24

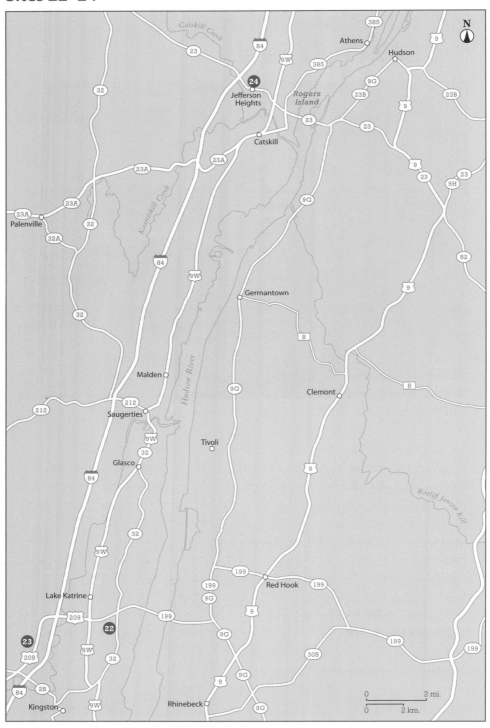

Highway 32 is very busy and parking is very limited along the highways.

Finding the site: Take US 209N to NY 199, and then take the exit for NY 32S. Go about 0.5 mile, and you will see a very small parking area on the left. Make a U-turn and park here. The outcrops are on the west side of Highway 32.

Rockhounding

The Kingston area has some very interesting exposures of carbonates and potential fossil sites, but I have found safe parking to be a significant challenge in the area. This site has a very small, relatively safe area for parking, but you still must cross the highway to get to the mineralized zones. The calcite mineralization is also somewhat limited, but I have found some areas with platy calcite crystals that are well exposed in outcrop. It would take some significant work with a hammer and chisel to extract these zones, but it is also possible to find some loose pieces with crystals on the ground as well. My time at this locality was limited since it was a late afternoon visit. I also found some fossils in loose rocks on the ground, but did not encounter any significant fossils in the outcrops.

References: Zabriskie, 2006

23. Kingston Highway 209 Fossils

Brachiopods are the most common fossil at this site.

(See map on page 78.)

County: Ulster

Site type: Cliffs along highway

Land status: Uncertain, not posted

Material: Fossils

Host rock: Shales of Devonian Lower Hamilton Group

Difficulty: Easy

Family-friendly: No, fossils very sparse

Tools needed: Hammer, chisel, flat-bladed screwdriver

Special concerns: Ticks, traffic outside of parking areas

Special attractions: Catskill Mountains

GPS parking: N41° 57' 42" / W74° 01' 24"

Topographic quadrangle: Kingston West, NY

Finding the site: From I-87, take exit 19 towards NY 28W. Take NY 28 and proceed about 0.4 mile, then take US 209N for approximately 2.2 miles. Take the Sawmill Road exit, turn left, and proceed to the ramp to US 209S. Go 1.2 miles and look for

Fossils can be found near the base of the cliffs in the talus.

the second broad turnoff to the right. Parking is well off the road in this area, and it can get muddy if it rains.

Rockhounding

These cliffs expose shales of the middle-to-late Devonian Lower Hamilton Group. Many of the shales are barren, and it takes some effort to find rocks with fossils. I had my best luck along the base of the cliffs and looked for loose rocks that had cracks, voids, and other indications of potential fossil-bearing zones. The best way to find the fossils is to use your hammer to break open the rocks, and use the flat blade of a screwdriver to split the rocks along bedding planes. The fossil-bearing rocks were also usually much darker and had minor iron staining when compared to the rocks without fossils. There are almost certainly some in-place beds of fossils along the cliffs, but I did not see any bedded zones. The fossils that I found were limited to small brachiopods and casts of shells, but small rugose horn corals are also reported to be present in this area.

References: United States Geological Survey, 2003

24. Catskill Highway 23 Taconic Unconformity

Silurian rocks are tilted and overlay even more tilted Ordovician rocks at this unconformity.

(See map on page 78.)

County: Greene

Site type: Roadcut

Land status: Uncertain, not posted

Material: Sandy dolomite, shale, and sandstone

Host rock: Ordovician Austin Glen and Silurian Rondout Formations

Difficulty: Easy

Family-friendly: Yes, but better for adults and older kids

Tools needed: None

Special concerns: No collecting, traffic, parking well off the road

Special attractions: Catskill Mountains Parks

GPS parking: N42° 14' 21" / W73° 53' 09"

Topographic quadrangle: Cementon, NY

Finding the site: This is a relatively easy site to find, but it takes a roundabout route to get there since it is next to a one-way on-ramp. From I-87, take exit 21 to NY 23 to Catskill. Turn left onto Main Street and proceed about 1.7 miles southeast, then take the ramp to Tannersville/Hunter. Take a sharp left onto US 9W N, and continue to follow this for about 0.5 mile. Take the NY 23W ramp to Cairo, keep right at the fork, and merge onto NY 23W. Continue 1.2 miles, and take the ramp to Jefferson Heights/Leeds. The roadcut will be approximately 260 feet farther on your right (northeast). Pull as far off the shoulder as possible. This site is best seen on early mornings on weekends or other times when the traffic is light.

Rockhounding

This is a classic locality that shows a significant angular unconformity, and it is often referred to as the "Taconic Unconformity." At this site tilted sandy dolomites of the Late Silurian Rondout Formation lay unconformably on truncated and nearly vertical beds of shales and sandstones of the Middle Ordovician Austin Glen Formation. The Austin Glen Formation formed approximately 465 million years ago, while the Rondout Formation is approximately 420 million years old. These numbers are very approximate, and it is difficult to really comprehend the age of these rocks and the time represented by their deposition and subsequent mountain-building events. However, one thing that is very clear is that there is a significant amount of time between the development of these two formations, and a rough estimate is approximately 45 million years. The beds of the Austin Glen formation were folded and eroded during an earlier tectonic event during the Taconic Orogeny, which subsided about 440 million years ago. The beds of Rondout Formation were laid down horizontally and then all the rocks were tilted again during a subsequent tectonic event during the Acadian Orogeny, which lasted from approximately 375 to 325 million years ago. When you look at this roadcut, try to comprehend the vastness of time represented by the uncon-formity itself, which is "only" about 45 million years, and then try to put into perspective the relative ages of the formations and the tectonic events that resulted in this roadcut. It is actually quite challenging and gives you a sense of what is really meant by geologic time.

References: Bennington, 2008; Stoffer and Messina, 2003

25. Stark's Knob Pillow Basalts and Pyrite

This piece of pyrite was found on the adjacent pit in the Normanskill Shale.

County: Saratoga
Site type: Former quarry and borrow pit
Land status: New York State Museum Natural History Site
Material: Pillow basalt at Stark's Knob, pyrite in adjacent borrow pit
Host rock: Pillow basalts at Stark's Knob and fractured shale/slate in borrow pit
Difficulty: Easy, but no collecting at Stark's Knob
Family-friendly: Yes
Tools needed: None
Special concerns: No collecting, uncertain status of borrow pit
Special attractions: Hudson River
GPS parking: N43° 07' 06" / W73°35' 07"
GPS Stark's Knob: N43° 07' 07" / W73° 35' 15"
Topographic quadrangle: Schuylerville, NY

Sites 25–26

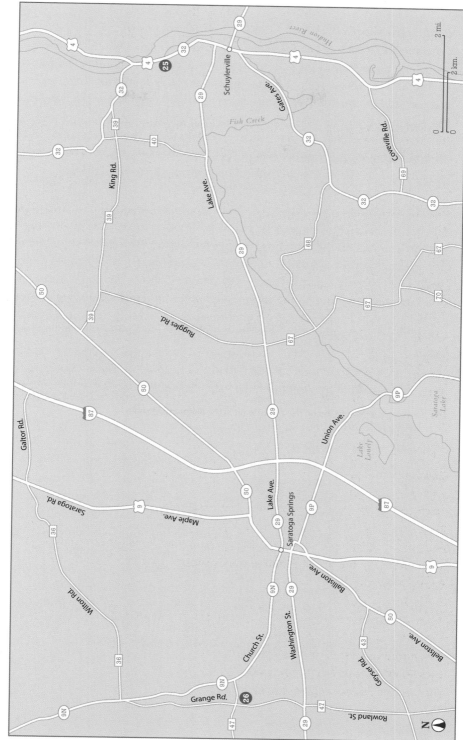

Finding the site: From I-87, take exit 14 for NY 9P towards NY 29E to Schuylerville. Continue about 9.2 miles and turn left (north) onto NY 32. Continue 1.1 miles north, and turn left onto Starks Knob Road. The parking area is immediately to your right, and is easy to spot as it has historical marker signs. From here, walk west on Starks Knob Road for approximately 350 feet, past the first driveway to the right, and then walk north along a faint path to the quarry area. There are three descriptive signs next to the quarry at Starks Knob. The borrow pit is located approximately 450 feet northeast of the Starks Knob quarry, and can be reached by parking on NY 32 on the west side of the highway adjacent to the site.

Rockhounding

Starks Knob is a former quarry in pillow basalts that formed about 460 to 440 million years ago in the Taconic Orogeny during the Ordovician. They are significant in that they are the only exposure of extrusive igneous rocks in New York. They were basalts that were extruded in shallow seas that formed "pillows" as they came out of the ground and were suddenly cooled by seawater.

In addition to their geologic significance, the knob played an important role in the Battle of Saratoga in 1777. General John Stark held the eastern portion of this hill along the Hudson River and kept the British from retreating. It later got the name Stark's Knob but not until long after the Revolutionary War. The basalts were well on their way to being quarried away for "road metal" up until about 1914. The site was donated to the American Scenic and Historic Preservation Society in 1916, and the site has recently been upgraded with signs and a parking area.

You can easily climb onto Stark's Knob to see the pillow basalts up close, but you cannot collect any rocks from this area. The pillows are fairly distinct and have an obvious rounded character. The small borrow pit to the east is reportedly in the Ordovician Normanskill Shale, and this shale is highly fractured and has some sections that are like long splinters. Nodules of pyrite can be found on the surface of the shale. This area is not posted, and it is not certain if this is part of the Stark's Knob educational site, so I am uncertain about both the collecting and access status of this area. It is certainly not part of the pillow basalts, but still has some interesting fractured shale and pyrite.

References: Cushing and Ruedemann, 1914; Isachsen, 1965

26. Lester Park Stromatolites

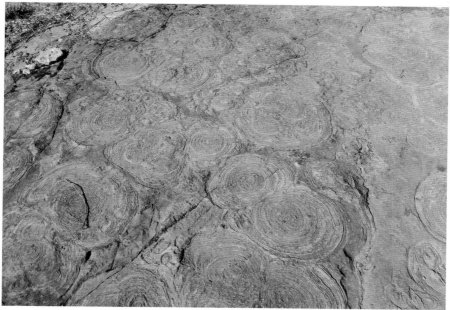

These stromatolites are a few inches to about one foot in diameter.

(See map on page 85.)
County: Saratoga
Site type: Roadside educational park
Land status: New York State Museum
Material: Stromatolites in outcrop
Host rock: Hoyt Limestone
Difficulty: Easy
Family-friendly: Yes
Tools needed: None
Special concerns: Educational site only, no collecting
Special attractions: Adirondack Mountains
GPS parking: N43° 05' 31" / W73° 50' 53"
Topographic quadrangle: Saratoga Springs, NY
Finding the site: From I-87, take exit 15 for NY 50 towards NY 29. Keep right at the fork and merge onto NY 29 Truck W/NY 50S. Proceed 2 miles, then turn right

The stromatolites form distinct mounds in the limestone.

onto NY 9N/Church Street and continue 2.9 miles. Turn left onto CR 21/Middle Grove Road, go 0.5 mile, and turn left (south) onto Lester Park Road. Proceed 0.2 mile. The parking area will be on your left. Note that Lester Park Road is sometimes referred to as Petrified Gardens Road.

Rockhounding

This roadside park is an excellent place to see stromatolites in outcrop. It is owned by the New York State Museum, and has some informational boards at the site. It is just north of another site known as Petrified Gardens, which unfortunately was closed at the time of my visit to the area in early May 2013. The stromatolites are the fossils of blue-green algae mats that formed on the sea floor nearly 500 million years ago. The host rock is the late Cambrian Hoyt limestone. Stromatolites are sometimes referred to as fossil "cabbage heads" or "brussel sprouts." While relatively common in Cambrian limestones, it is relatively rare to have such an accessible roadside exposure where you can easily see the stromatolites so well exposed.

References: Halley, 1971; Zabriskie, 1999.

27. Canajoharie Creek Fossils

Fossils can be found in the hillside near this boulder with ribbons of travertine.

County: Montgomery
Site type: Creek bed and bank outcrops
Land status: Uncertain, may be city land, not posted except upstream at dam
Material: Brachiopods, bryozoan, fossil "hash"
Host rock: Middle Ordovician Trenton Limestone and Utica Formation black shale
Difficulty: Moderate
Family-friendly: Yes, very pleasant place to visit, but no swimming
Tools needed: Hammer, chisel
Special concerns: No-trespassing zone north of upstream dam
Special attractions: "Dummy" traffic light, one of three left in the United States
GPS parking: N42° 53' 53" / W74° 34' 16"
GPS fossil outcrop: N42° 53' 51" / W74° 34' 13"
Topographic quadrangle: Canajoharie, NY
Finding the site: This is actually an easy site to find, but you have to drive through downtown Canajoharie. From I-90, take exit 29 to US 10S. Turn right (west) onto

Sites 27–29

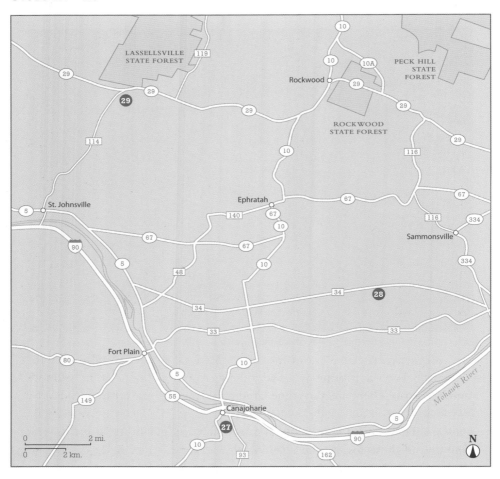

East Main Street, go about 0.2 mile, and turn left (south) onto Mitchell Street. Go about 400 feet and turn right (southeast) onto Moyer Street. Proceed 0.3 mile and take the second right (south) onto Floral Avenue. Follow Floral Avenue south to the small parking area, which is a public access point to the creek. From here, follow the trail to Canajoharie Creek.

Rockhounding

This is a beautiful spot for just a hike, even if you are not collecting fossils. This area is near the boundary between the Hudson-Mohawk Lowlands and

Canajoharie Creek itself is a worthwhile place to visit.

the Allegheny Plateau. Most of the fossils that I found here were in the hillside just below the parking area, and these were a fossil "hash" of brachiopods and bryozoan. There are also some large boulders with travertine in this area. Farther upstream the flat beds of the black shale of the Utica Formation are exposed. These shales reportedly have trilobites and graptolites, but I did not find any of these fossils. The dam upstream is posted against trespassing, so do not go into this area. The area is also posted against swimming, which is unfortunate as the creek has creek potholes that formed in the limestone of the creek bed. Local law enforcement reportedly takes the "no swimming" policy very seriously. There are no indications that fossil collecting is prohibited, but confine your collecting to loose rocks and do not damage any prominent outcrops.

References: Zabriskie, 2006

28. Diamond Acres Herkimer Diamonds

This small Herkimer was found in the dolostone of the southern tailings pile.

(See map on page 90.)

County: Montgomery

Site type: Open pits, fee collecting

Land status: Private

Material: Herkimer diamonds and anthraxolite

Host rock: Cambrian Little Falls Dolostone

Difficulty: Easy to extremely hard

Family-friendly: Yes

Tools needed: Sledgehammer, hammer, chisel, shovel, gloves, and safety glasses

Special concerns: No facilities, rural location, lunch and supplies needed

Special attractions: None

GPS entrance: N42° 57' 51" / W74° 28' 31"

GPS south tailings: N42° 57' 43" / W74° 28' 30"

Claims at Diamond Acres are marked by ropes, and the excavations give you a sense of the effort needed to find the best Herkimer diamonds.

Topographic quadrangle: Randall, NY
Finding the site: From I-90, take exit 28 towards NY 30A, Fultonville/Fonda. Turn left (west) on Riverside Drive, go 0.6 mile, and then turn right (north) onto Main Street. Cross the Mohawk River, and continue onto Bridge Street about 0.3 mile. Turn left (right) on NY 5W/East Main Street, go about 0.9 mile, and take a slight right (northwest) onto Hickory Hill Road. Go 1.5 miles, and turn right (north) onto Martin Road. Continue for 0.3 mile and take the fork to the left (northwest) onto Stone Arabia Road. Continue 3.2 miles, and the entrance is on your left (south). It is approximately 800 feet past the intersection of England Road (to the north) and Barker Road (to the south). The address is 1706 Stone Arabia Rd., Fonda, NY 12068. The entrance is a small unpaved drive and is easy to miss, but there is plenty of parking for the site once you leave the highway.

Rockhounding

This site is in Montgomery County, not Herkimer County, and consequently is not visited as much by the tourists that come to look for Herkimer "diamonds." Herkimer diamonds, commonly referred to as "Herkimers," are actually quartz crystals, but they are very clear and have a high refractive index. This gives them the appearance of diamonds, and they are very popular as semi-precious gemstones. This site is well known among Herkimer miners, and many miners have active claims at this site. The daily collecting fee is extremely reasonable, and much of the area still has a lot of trees, which provide some very good shade during hot days. Children and pets are welcome, and the rules for digging are very reasonable, with emphasis on responsible digging and keeping the area clean. The owner has worked very hard to preserve the trees and as much of the natural environment as possible while still allowing digging for Herkimers. You can lease a claim at the site for a yearly fee, but it must be worked at least once every fourteen days or you forfeit the claim. This is a very good rule as it makes sure that the claims are actively worked and keeps absentee owners from locking up a site. There are often people waiting for a claim, so if you lose your claim, you may not get the same spot back. It is also important to note that from October 1 to May 1, digging is restricted to claim owners only.

During my visit to the site in May 2013, the site had an area of northern and southern workings. I spent most of my time in the southern workings, which are in the woods. I stayed well out of the claim areas, which are clearly marked with ropes, and focused on the tailings outside of the claims piles. I did not have a sledgehammer and was limited to my rock hammer, but I was still able to break open some rocks and find some vugs with small Herkimers and calcite. The site also has anthraxolite (a very beautiful mineral name), which is a bitumenlike substance that may be related to Cambrian algal mats. I have seen similar occurrences of this black material in dolostones of similar ages, so if you come across a tarlike substance in the dolostones, it is likely the anthraxolite. I also saw a shredded fiberglass handle of a sledge hammer on the tailings, which gave me an indication of how tough it is to break apart the dolostone. You can find some good crystals in the tailings, but like all Herkimer sites, it takes a lot of hard work. You must be extremely careful when breaking apart the rocks as flying rock chips and steel can be quite dangerous.

References: Walter, 2004; Zabriskie, 2006

29. Crystal Grove Herkimer Diamonds

The serious miners work the low walls with steel wedges and hand tools to remove large slabs of dolostone and expose pockets of Herkimers.

(See map on page 90.)

County: Fulton

Site type: Open pit, fee collecting

Land status: Private, fee

Material: Herkimer Diamonds, anthraxolite, calcite, and dolomite

Host rock: Cambrian Little Falls Dolostone

Difficulty: Easy to extremely difficult

Family-friendly: Yes

This is a Herkimer that just came out of a pocket that was found by a miner in the low walls of the Tears of Wenedi pit.

Tools needed: Sledgehammer, hammer, chisel, shovel, gloves, and safety glasses

Special concerns: Proper tools and safety equipment

Special attractions: Fort Klock, Saranac-Utica Brewery Tour

GPS parking for shop: N43° 03' 00" / W74° 38' 11"

GPS parking for mines: N43° 03' 4" / W74° 38' 1"

Topographic quadrangle: Oppenheim, NY

Finding the site: The best way to get to the site is to start in St. Johnsville, which is best accessed through NY 5, as there is no direct highway from I-90 across the Mohawk River. From St. Johnsville, head north on North Division Street for 0.8 mile and then take a slight right (northeast) onto Lassellsville Road. Continue on Lasselsville Road, which is CR 56, for 1.1 miles; it will change into CR 114. Continue 2.5 miles, and look for the entrance to Crystal Grove on your right. The address is 161 County Hwy 114, St. Johnsville, NY 13452.

Rockhounding

This is an excellent site with easy access to find Herkimer diamonds. Pay at the shop and drive to the mine sites. As of May 2013, the site had two main mining areas, which were the Tears of Wenedi Mine and the Black Diamond Mine. Both mines are very broad open pits and do not present significant fall hazards. I was provided a site map, which was very helpful. I spent most of my time in the Tears of Wenedi mine, which was fairly crowded with both casual collectors and serious miners. The Black Diamond mine did not have anyone in the pit, which indicated to me that my time was best spent with the other miners in the Wenedi pit, as they were obviously finding Herkimers.

The Wenedi mine had several serious miners working the very low walls of the mine. The miners would take large steel wedges to break apart the rocks, and this would ultimately expose some pockets. I say ultimately because they often have to break through several layers of the dolostone, and this is some of the hardest rock to break apart with hand tools. I focused on break-ing apart some of the rocks in the waste rock piles, and was able to find some pieces with broken Herkimers. I also found some loose crystals on the ground. The good thing about this site, if you have kids, is that they can find loose crystals on the ground and in some of the loose rocks. The site is only as difficult as you decide to make it.

Crystal Grove has a campground as well, and the site is open seven days a week from April 15 to October 15. Digging hours are from 9 a.m. to 7 p.m., which is a big help as I often like to work into the late afternoon, and some of the other Herkimer sites end their digging times at 5 p.m. While the shop has some snacks, it does not have a restaurant or grocery store, so you should also make sure to either bring a lunch or eat before you come to the mine. Once you start looking for the diamonds you are not going to want to stop.

References: Zabriskie, 2006

30. Herkimer Diamond Mines

This is the north end of Mine 3 at the Herkimer Diamond Mines.

County: Herkimer

Site type: Quarry, fee-collecting

Land status: Private

Material: Herkimer diamonds

Host rock: Cambrian Little Falls Dolostone

Difficulty: Easy to extremely difficult, depending on your expectations

Family-friendly: Yes

Tools needed: Sledgehammer, hammer, chisel, shovel, gloves, and safety glasses

Special concerns: Lots of work to find one crystal, not good for the impatient

Special attractions: Fishing in West Canada Creek

GPS parking: N43° 07' 42" / W74° 58' 35"

Topographic quadrangle: Middleville, NY

Finding the site: From I–90, take exit 30 towards NY 28. Follow the signs to take you to NY 28N, and proceed about 7.3 miles north. The parking lot and building

Sites 30–34

This Herkimer was found by breaking apart the dark gray vuggy rocks with a sledgehammer.

with the large Herkimer Diamond Mines sign will be on your left (west). The street address is 4601 State Route 28, Herkimer, NY 13350.

Rockhounding

This is a must stop if you are in the Herkimer area. The complex has an excellent shop, museum, and restrooms, and it is very easy to find and access. The mines are just north of the complex and are a short walk from the parking area. After you pay your fee, you also have the opportunity to see a short introductory video that gives you some guidance on finding the Herkimers. I highly recommend watching this before going to the mines. The video emphasizes that you should look for rocks with vugs and holes, as most of the solid rocks are just that—solid dolostone that is barren of crystals. The video also makes it clear that while you can find some Herkimers, you will have to work for them. I soon learned that they were absolutely correct about that part.

I started early in the morning in July, and I brought my sledgehammer as well as my regular hammer. There are three mines here, referred to as Mines One and Two (which have been combined) and Mine Three. I started at the north end of Mine Three. I broke apart several large rocks with my

This Herkimer broke out of a rock I was trimming, but fortunately I was able to find it on the ground.

sledgehammer but only found some dolomite crystals. I soon learned to look for the vuggy rocks and focus on them. When I broke these apart I found pockets, but still no crystals. I then walked to the area between Mine Three and Mines One and Two, just north of the small stream, and found an area with some broken rocks that were dark gray and vuggy. After breaking a few of the rocks, I exposed an excellent Herkimer, and shortly afterwards broke out a very small Herkimer that I was able to find on the ground; they were crystal clear and very impressive. If you come to this site, be prepared to work very hard, but you will almost certainly find some good Herkimers if you are persistent and make an effort to find the right rocks. Kids and adults that are not breaking apart rocks also have an excellent chance of finding good crystals on the ground, as long as you are in a zone that has crystals.

The site has a KOA Campground, a cafe, restaurant, and other nearby dining options. The mining areas are open April 15 through October 31 from 9 a.m. to 5 p.m. daily. I recommend starting early in the day if possible to beat the heat, take advantage of morning weather (afternoon showers are common), and to maximize your time collecting. The site is also next to a competing Herkimer site, the Ace of Diamonds Mine (Site 30), and I recommend visiting both sites if your time and budget permit.

References: Eckert, 2000

31. Ace of Diamonds Mine

This stockpile is regularly replenished with fresh material from the active mining operation on site.

(See map on page 98.)
County: Herkimer
Site type: Quarry, fee-collecting
Land status: Private
Material: Herkimer diamonds
Host rock: Cambrian Little Falls Dolostone
Difficulty: Easy to extremely difficult, depending on your expectations
Family-friendly: Yes
Tools needed: Sledgehammer, hammer, chisel, shovel, gloves, and safety glasses
Special concerns: Lots of work to find crystals, no guarantees
Special attractions: Fishing in West Canada Creek
GPS parking: N43° 07' 56" / W74° 58' 24"
Topographic quadrangle: Middleville, NY
Finding the site: From I-90, take exit 30 towards NY 28. Follow the signs to take you to NY 28N, and proceed about 7.6 miles north. A large orange sign that says ACE OF DIAMONDS MINE/HERKIMER DIAMONDS will be on your left (west). However, the

road to the parking area is a very sharp turn, and you cannot turn directly left. Proceed past the entrance, make a U-turn, and drive up the inclined road to the parking area and the mine. The street address is reportedly 84 Herkimer St., Middleville, NY 13350, and this will get you to the site, but based on Google Maps this is a little further north than the entrance.

Rockhounding

This is a great site and should also not be missed if you are in the Herkimer area. The office has an excellent bookstore and has several books on New York geology and minerals that are very hard to find. After paying the fee I was given a map and a description of what to expect. They have an area that they mine and regularly bring rocks up from the mining area to the large stockpile next to the office. I spent quite a bit of time at this stockpile and found some nice crystals. I also hiked up to the upper area, which had some rocks that had crystals of dolomite and calcite. These upper rocks were generally fractured and easier to break apart, but I did not find any good Herkimers in these rocks. They also have an area that they screen, and you can sometimes find crystals in the screenings. The area had quite a few miners and many people were focused on digging into the stockpile and screening for loose Herkimers.

Make sure you use your safety glasses, boots, a proper hammer, and heavy gloves when looking for Herkimers. I had just put my camera away and started breaking apart dolostones with my sledgehammer, and forgot to put on my heavy gloves. A sharp piece of dolostone shot off the rock and into the knuckle of the middle finger of my right hand. The blood stopped after a few minutes, but weeks later I still could not completely bend my finger. Another collector at this site noticed that my legs had also taken a beating, as I was wearing shorts, which is another bad idea if you are breaking apart dolos-tones. My lower legs had numerous gashes from flying dolostone, and blood was steadily dripping from the cuts. It did not hurt but it attracted a lot of mosquitoes, and it really hurt when I sprayed my bloody shins with bug spray.

The site is also next to a competing Herkimer site, the Herkimer Diamond Mines (Site 29), and I recommend visiting both sites if your time and budget permit. The Ace of Diamonds Mine is open April 1 to October 31 every day from 9 a.m. to 5 p.m. Campsites are available at the mine site. The site does not have a restaurant or food, but they are available within walking distance.

References: Eckert, 2000

32. Newville Nowadaga Creek Graptolites and Trilobites

This black shale has been split, and the white streaks in the shale are graptolite fossils.

(See map on page 98.)
County: Herkimer
Site type: Rocks in creek
Land status: Private, not posted
Material: Graptolites and trilobites
Host rock: Middle Ordovician Utica shale
Difficulty: Easy to moderate
Family-friendly: Yes, but land status possibly an issue
Tools needed: Flat-bladed screwdriver, hammer, chisel
Special concerns: Land status and access
Special attractions: None
GPS parking: N42° 59' 44" / W74° 47' 18"
Topographic quadrangle: Van Hornesville, NY
Finding the site: From I-90, take exit 29A towards NY 169, then turn left (west) to get onto NY 5S E. Continue on NY 5S E for 2.3 miles, then turn right (southwest)

The bed of Nowadaga Creek is beds of nearly horizontal Middle Ordovician Utica shale.

onto CR 102/Creek Road. Proceed to the first bridge over Nowadaga Creek, and park on the west side of the road just before you cross the bridge. The south bank of the creek is posted against trespassing but I did not see any "no trespassing" signs on the north bank, so I stayed on the north bank. The rocks with the graptolites and trilobites are in the creek bed.

Rockhounding

This site offers the opportunity to find graptolites and trilobites in the Utica shale. The best collecting appears to be downstream from the bridge. There are many large pieces of black Utica shale lying on the west bank that can be split open. Many of these pieces have abundant graptolites, and they can easily be seen on both fresh and weathered surfaces of the black shale. The trilobites can be found in a similar way. I found many more graptolites than trilobites, and the trilobites that I found were generally in fragments and very small. Trilobites can reportedly be found in other sections of Nowadaga Creek, and I explored some other areas farther upstream, but did not find any. Much of the stream is also posted against trespassing, so you need to be very careful to stay out of posted land. The site described here, while not posted, is undoubtedly private so it is probably not a good site for large groups. It is definitely a locality that is frequented by rockhounds, however. I saw lots of examples of freshly broken rock and also found a small chisel on the bridge, which I left hoping that the original owner would be able to return to retrieve it.

References: Zabriskie, 2006

33. Ilion Jerusalem Hill Road Orange Travertine

This orange travertine was found near the road washout.

(See map on page 98.)

County: Herkimer

Site type: Boulders in stream gorge

Land status: Uncertain, may be town property

Material: Orange travertine

Host rock: Late Silurian dark red-brown shale

Difficulty: Easy

Family-friendly: Yes

Tools needed: Hammer, chisel. Sledgehammer may be useful for large boulders

Special concerns: Some hiking, next to creek, poison ivy

Special attractions: Herkimer diamond sites

GPS parking: N42° 57' 43" / W75° 06' 12"

GPS travertine at road washout: N42° 57' 48" / W75° 06' 41"

Topographic quadrangle: Millers Mills, NY

The travertine can be found all along the stream, and some of the best pieces are just east of the road washout.

Finding the site: From I-90, take exit 30 for NY 28, and turn left (south) onto Mohawk Street, and then turn right (west) onto NY 5S. Go about 1.7 miles and take the NY 51 exit towards Ilion. Follow NY 51 south 5.9 miles to the parking area, which is on the right at a closed gate that says ROAD CLOSED. This is Jerusalem Hill Road according to local road maps, but it is not marked as such in the field. Park here, and walk approximately 2,000 feet upstream to where the road is washed out. The travertine is found as large boulders and rocks in the stream.

Rockhounding

This site offers the opportunity to find large pieces of orange travertine. Some collectors have found very large pieces, but most of the pieces that I found were aggregates of relatively small, translucent, orange pieces of travertine. The travertine occurs as precipitates and generally has a rounded smooth appearance as opposed to having prominent bands. The boulders in the creek were surprisingly hard and difficult to break. In addition to the area of the road washout, you can find lots of pieces of travertine downstream. The creek banks can be steep and slippery, so be very careful if you look along the sides of the gorge.

During my trip to the site in July 2013, NY 51 was closed due to the extreme damage caused by flooding earlier that summer. However, I was able to use my GPS to go around the closed area and approached the parking area from the south. Using my GPS kept this trip from becoming a bust and demonstrated the usefulness of having a backup plan in case an access road is unexpectedly closed.

References: Walter, 2004; Rogers et al., 1990

34. Forge Hollow Travertine

This is a freshy broken surface on a typical piece of travertine from this site.

(See map on page 98.)
County: Oneida County
Site type: Waterfall on roadside
Land status: Uncertain, not posted
Material: Travertine
Host rock: Upper Silurian Dolomites of the Bertie Group
Difficulty: Easy
Family-friendly: Yes
Tools needed: Hammer, chisel
Special concerns: Traffic on roadside, wet conditions
Special attractions: None
GPS parking: N42° 57' 31" / W75° 24' 20"
Topographic quadrangle: Oriskany Falls, NY
Finding the site: From I-90, take exit 32 towards NY 233, and head south for approximately 6.4 miles. Turn right (southwest) onto NY 12B S, and go 3 miles. Turn left (east) onto NY 315E, and continue 2.9 miles to the site on the right

White and light tan travertine can be found at the base of the waterfall.

(south) side of the road. A waterfall marks the location of the travertine, and there is adequate parking on the side of the road.

Rockhounding

I originally came to this site to look for Eurypterid fossils, as the Forge Hollow area is a reported eurypterid locality. West of the waterfall are some flat carbonate rocks in outcrop, but unfortunately I did not find any fossils in them. However, I noticed that the waterfall adjacent to the parking area had considerable travertine around its base. The travertine appears to have formed very recently, and is generally white with some tan areas on the inside. While this travertine is not as extensive as the travertine deposits in the Ilion Gorge, it still is interesting to check out, and it is a very easy site to find and visit. The only issue is that you may get wet when you cross the small drainage between the road and the waterfall. During periods of rain the waterfall may also get much bigger, and care must be taken to avoid any debris that may fall from the waterfall.

References: Rickard, 1955; Fisher, 1959

35. Batchellerville Pegmatites

This is a large mica book and orange microcline found near the intersection of the road with Gordons Creek.

County: Saratoga
Site type: Road with minerals
Land status: Private, signs say STAY ON TRAIL
Material: Muscovite, biotite, microcline
Host rock: Pegmatites in gneiss
Difficulty: Easy
Family-friendly: Yes
Tools needed: None
Special concerns: Private land adjacent to road
Special attractions: None
GPS parking: N43° 14' 24" / W74° 03' 48"
GPS road intersection with Gordons Creek: N43° 14' 17" / W74° 03' 10"
Topographic quadrangle: Edinburg, NY

Sites 35–38

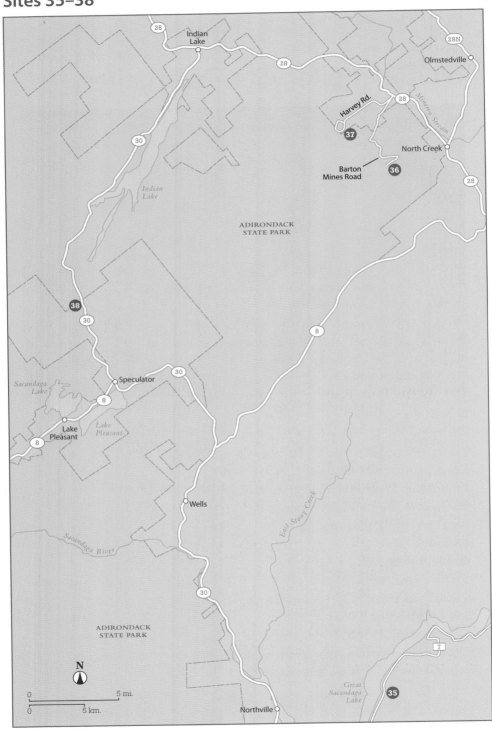

28
Indian Lake
28N
28
Olmstedville
Harvey Rd.
28
Minerva Stream
30
37
North Creek
Indian Lake
Barton Mines Road
36
28
ADIRONDACK STATE PARK
38
30
8
30
Speculator
Sacandaga Lake
8
Lake Pleasant
Lake Pleasant
8
Wells
East Stony Creek
Sacandaga River
30
ADIRONDACK STATE PARK
7
N
Great Sacandaga Lake
35
0   5 mi.
0   5 km.
Northville

Finding the site: From I-90, take exit 27 to NY 30, and continue 9.2 miles to CR 155. As you continue on this road for 1.1 miles, CR 155 turns into Main Street, and then North Street, and then CR 110. Continue another 7.9 miles and the road turns into CR 7, which is South Shore Road. Continue another 4.7 miles and you will come to a large bridge to your left (west) that crosses Great Sacandaga Lake. This is NY 98, but you do not take this bridge. Stay on the east shore of Great Sacandaga Lake on CR 7, and continue 2.4 miles to a small road that has a sign indicating that it is Mine Road. Turn right (east) onto Mine Road, and continue east to the parking area, which is next to a house and located just west of where the road becomes much rougher. Park off to the side to make sure that you do not block the road. The road is not paved, and you can see lots of minerals on the surface.

Rockhounding

The Batchellerville pegmatites were first worked in 1906 for high-quality microcline for the ceramics industry. The coarse muscovite of the pegmatites was also mined and an attempt was made to use it for dielectric material, but micro-granular iron and staining made it unsuitable for electrical applications. Mining was continuous until 1921 and was sporadic until it ceased entirely around 1934.

The mines are located on the sides of Mine Road as you head north from the parking area. The mines are on private property, and you should not leave the road unless you have permission. One of the signs along the road says STAY ON THE TRAIL, RESPECT THE LANDOWNER. Fortunately, you do not have to leave the road at all. There is plenty of muscovite, biotite, and coarse orange microcline along the road. Many of the granitic rocks also have graphic inter-growths, and these types of rocks are often called "graphic granite."

The road forks just before it crosses Gordons Creek, and additional mines are reported to be present on the left (west) fork of the road. We saw a large water-filled pit just west of this road, and lots of mica and feldspar adjacent to it. There was also previous mining activity at the location of the fork, as the woods appear to have grown over the mine dumps. The creek at the road intersection is full of rocks with large books of mica and orange microcline. Many other miner-als, such as beryl, chrysoberyl, and garnet are also reported at the Batchellerville Pegmatites, but we did not find any of these minerals. Closer inspection of some of the rocks in the road may reveal their presence, but we were more than happy with the large mica books and orange microcline that we found along the road.

References: Zabriskie, 2006; Tan, 1966; Newland, 1919

36. Barton Mines Garnet

Excellent hand samples can be easily found in the collecting area.

(See map on page 110.)
County: Warren
Site type: Former mine
Land status: Private, fee collecting
Material: Dark red garnet
Host rock: Gabbro and anorthosite
Difficulty: Easy
Family-friendly: Yes
Tools needed: None, except for small plastic bags
Special concerns: No hammering allowed, must pay by pound for rocks, not open until late June
Special attractions: Hudson River rafting and nearby Hooper garnet mine
GPS parking shop: N43° 41' 16" / W74° 03' 32"
GPS parking mine: N43° 40' 49" / W74° 03' 19"
Topographic quadrangle: Thirteenth Lake, NY

The ground is rich in deep red-brown garnet fragments.

Finding the site: From I-87, take exit 23 towards Warrensburg. Turn left onto Diamond Point Road, go 0.2 mile, and turn right (north) on US 9N. Proceed 4.2 miles, and turn left (northwest) onto NY 28. Continue 20.6 miles to the small hamlet of North River, and turn left (west) onto Barton Mines Road. Follow this road 4.7 miles to the shop, which is on the right.

Rockhounding

The Barton Mines near Gore Mountain are world famous for their distinctive garnet. It is easily recognizable, as it is very dark red, has a resinous luster, and exhibits right-angle fracturing. This fracturing pattern, combined with its hardness, makes the Barton garnets superb abrasives. Every rockhound should visit this site at least once to collect some of this unique garnet. Garnet was named the New York state gem in 1969.

The mine tour starts with a very brief history of the deposit. In 1846, Henry Hudson Barton came to Boston and apprenticed as a jeweler. A person came to his operation with some garnets to cut into gems, but Barton could not properly cut the stones. They would often fracture into sharp pieces and were not gem quality. Several years later he was working in Philadelphia and became involved with abrasives and sandpaper for woodworking. The sandpaper they used was made from ground glass and quartz, and did not cut well. Barton then remembered the garnets he had been shown, and went to New York to find their source. He soon found the garnets and discovered that they made an excellent abrasive and sandpaper. Barton started mining the garnets

Pouring water over the garnet-rich ground is the recommended method to get quality garnets.

in 1878 and purchased all of Gore Mountain in 1887. Mining was largely done by hand tools, and the site was modernized in 1924 with a mill and steam tools. The pit closed in the 1980s when the water table was intersected and the mines flooded. The Barton mines operation was then moved to Ruby Mountain to the north, and the company still produces garnet. Fortunately, they have kept the original pit open to collectors on a fee basis, and it is set up as a very safe and accessible family-friendly site.

Collecting at the former garnet pit is different than at most fee-mining sites, since hammering is not allowed. This is a good thing as the garnets are extremely sharp, and they fracture easily. If hammering was allowed the mine floor would soon become shattered garnet and they would undoubtedly have people injured by flying garnet shards. You can pick hand samples off the ground, but their recommended method is to take a bucket of water from the adjacent mine pond and pour it over the loose soil. Small washed fragments of garnets can then be easily seen and picked from the ground and put in a plastic bag. My preference was to look on the surface for the larger garnets, and I obtained some nice pieces that only cost a few additional dollars.

References: Bartolome, 1960; Robinson and Chamberlain, 2007

37. Hooper Mine Garnets

This massive piece of garnet was found by breaking apart a much larger rock.

(See map on page 110.)
County: Warren
Site type: Former garnet quarry
Land status: Part of Adirondack Park state land, access through private land
Material: Garnets
Host rock: Gneiss
Difficulty: Easy
Family-friendly: Yes
Tools needed: Sledgehammer, hammer, chisel
Special concerns: Permission needed from Garnet Hill Lodge
Special attractions: Garnet Hill Lodge
GPS parking: N43° 42' 36" / W74° 06' 19"
GPS mine: N43° 42' 30" / W74° 06' 01"
Topographic quadrangle: Thirteenth Lake, NY
Finding the site: From I-87, take exit 23 towards Warrensburg. Turn left onto Diamond Point Road, go 0.2 mile and turn right (north) on US 9N. Proceed 4.2

miles, and turn left (northwest) onto NY 28. Continue 21.2 miles through the small hamlet of North River, and turn left (west) onto Thirteenth Lake Road. Take this road 1 mile and turn left (southwest) onto Harvey Road. Continue on Harvey Road for 2.3 miles, and then it becomes Old Farm Road. Continue 0.3 mile, and take a slight left (south) onto 4-H Road. Continue on 4-H Road 0.6 mile to the parking area. Before you reach the parking area, stop in at the Garnet Hill Lodge, which is reached by a left turn approximately 0.4 mile after you turn onto 4-H Road. The Garnet Hill Lodge is approximately 0.2 mile from this turn. Ask for permission at the Lodge to visit the mine, and you may also be able to get a map showing the way. Drive to the parking area, which is reached by driving to the area of the ski shop near the tennis court. Park in this area, and walk up the road to the Old Mine Trail. You can drive up this road but the house at the end is a private residence, and you do not want to bother them, and there is no parking there. As you walk towards this house, you will see a faint path that leads up the hill, but it appears to double back towards the road. Follow this path; when it goes up the hill it becomes the path to the mine. The trail has some markers, but they are easy to miss. It is about a quarter-mile hike to the mine, and it is a moderately strenuous hike.

Rockhounding

The Hooper garnet mine was opened by Frank Hooper in 1889, and it was just north of the Barton Mines (Site 36). Unfortunately for Mr. Hooper, the garnets at his mine were much smaller and they could not compete with the Barton garnets. Hooper went to work for Mr. Barton, and the Hooper mine was abandoned as a garnet mine. The Garnet Hill Lodge has been very gracious in giving permission to cross their site to visit this mine, and this is certainly appreciated by the rockhound and geologist community. I hope they have generated some additional business from the visitors who come to the mine.

The rocks are Precambrian gneisses with moderately sized garnets. The garnets tend to break with the rock, so you do not have many garnets that form as distinct crystals. The best pieces seem to come from freshly broken surfaces, as the weathered surfaces are generally iron stained and not as attractive. It is very easy to find pieces with large garnets, but they are much smaller than the garnets at Gore Mountain. It is not hard to see why Mr. Barton drove Mr. Hooper out of business.

References: Miller, 1912

38. Speculator Highway 30 Diopside and Garnet

This is the brown garnet from the calc-silicate skarn next to the Pig Rock.

(See map on page 110.)

County: Hamilton

Site type: Roadcut

Land status: Uncertain, not posted

Material: Dark green diopside and brown garnet

Host rock: Calc-silicate skarn

Difficulty: Easy

Family-friendly: Yes, but not many rocks at base of cliff

Tools needed: Hammer, chisel

Special concerns: Limited collecting, ticks, mosquitoes, ants

Special attractions: None

GPS parking: N43° 33' 55" / W74° 23' 54"

GPS roadcut: N43° 33' 52" / W74° 23' 48"

Topographic quadrangle: Page Mountain, NY

This site is extremely easy to find thanks to the "Pig Rock" just east of the roadcut.

Finding the site: This is one of the easiest sites to find in this guidebook thanks to the artist(s) who painted the "Pig Rock" on the east side of NY 30. From the town of Speculator, take NY 30N from its intersection with NY 8. Proceed 5.1 miles, and you will see an outcrop on the east side of the road painted like the head of a pig. The best parking area is a small road to the left (west) side of NY 30, where you can pull off without blocking the road traffic. From here you can walk to the outcrop.

Rockhounding

This site is a calc-silicate skarn that is almost entirely fine-grained, dark green diopside. Large bands of brown garnet and veinlets of calcite can be seen in the outcrop. Surprisingly, there are not many loose rocks at the base of the outcrop, and if you collect material at this site you will likely have to hit it with a hammer. A small chisel can also be useful to break off fractured parts of the outcrop. However, make sure that you do not cause damage to the outcrop and confine your collecting to zones where the rock is already partially fractured. The brown garnet bands are relatively easy to see, but it is apparent that the easy-to-reach rocks were collected long ago. The outcrop is very steep and is not safe to climb, and it is also very high, so climbing up to the top from the lower areas is not recommended.

References: Zabriskie, 2006; Valentino et al., 2008

39. Brant Lake Roadcut Quartz Crystals

Quartz crystals can be found along fractures in the gneiss.

County: Warren
Site type: Outcrops on roadside
Land status: Uncertain, not posted
Material: Quartz crystals
Host rock: Gneiss and migmatite
Difficulty: Easy
Family-friendly: Yes, but very small area
Tools needed: Hammer, chisel
Special concerns: Traffic on road, limited amount of rocks for collecting
Special attractions: Brant Lake
GPS parking: N43° 44' 21" / W73° 40' 21"
Topographic quadrangle: Brant Lake, NY
Finding the site: From I-87, take exit 25 for NY 8 towards Chestertown/Hague. Turn right (east) on NY 8, and proceed 7.5 miles to CR 26 (Palisades Road). Turn left

Sites 39–47

The outcrop with the quartz crystals is easy to spot as the rocks are broken apart and much lighter in color than the unbroken barren gneisses.

(north), and proceed about 0.6 mile to the site. It can be seen on the right (east) side of road, and is distinguished by the pile of broken rocks next to the unbroken outcrops of gneiss. It will be necessary to make a U-turn to park along the wide area of the roadside on the west side of the road. You can then cross the road to get to the roadcut.

Rockhounding

This is a very small outcrop that has seen a number of rockhounds. I originally came to this area to find a reported occurrence of uvite, mica pseudomorphs after diopside, and graphite, but found that most of the outcrops in the area were barren coarse-grained gneiss. However, at this roadcut the rocks are broken apart, and there are seams of quartz crystals along some of the boulders. The crystals generally have a light coating of yellow-tan iron oxide and are well terminated. I did not see any uvite, mica, or graphite, but the quartz crystals make this a site that is well worth a stop. The site also has reasonably safe parking, which is always a concern when looking at minerals in roadcuts. Due to the limited size of the outcrop, it is very easy to overcollect at this site, so if you do decide to collect some quartz crystals, be sure to leave plenty for the next visitors to see.

References: Robinson and Chamberlain, 2007

40. Rock Pond Mine Sulfides

The dump next to Rock Pond is full of rocks with disseminated sulfides.

(See map on page 120.)
County: Essex County
Site type: Mine adit and dump
Land status: Pharaoh Lake Wilderness, Putnam Pond Campground
Material: Disseminated sulfides on mine dump
Host rock: Mica schists
Difficulty: Easy
Family-friendly: Yes, but will require a significant hike
Tools needed: None
Special concerns: No collecting, long strenuous hike
Special attractions: Pharaoh Lake Wilderness
GPS parking: N43° 50' 25" / W73° 34' 19"
GPS trailhead: N43° 50' 40" / W73° 34' 20"
GPS Rock Pond Mine: N43° 51' 15" / W73° 35' 26"
Topographic quadrangle: Graphite, NY
Finding the site: From I-87, take exit 28 for NY 74E, and proceed 12.5 miles. Turn right (south) onto CR 39/Putts Pond Road and continue 3.6 miles to the entrance

The Rock Pond Mine adit is right next to Rock Pond, and has a red discharge indicative of sulfide mineralization.

to Putnam Pond Campground. You will need to pay a vehicle fee. Park at the day-use area near the pond, and follow the trail north through the woods to the Heart Pond trailhead (which is confusing as you want to go to Rock Pond, not Heart Pond). This trailhead is right next to Campground 39. Follow this trail to the Rock Pond Mine, and closely watch the markers and signs as you hike. I strongly encourage you to get a map when you enter the campground. The staff at the gate did not have any information on where the trails start and could not help me with getting to the correct trailhead. I had to ask campers for directions.

Rockhounding

The Rock Pond Mine is often referred to as a graphite mine, but I did not see any indication of graphite at the site. There is a very small mine dump near Rock Pond, and this dump is loaded with dense rocks that are full of disseminated sulfides, which appear to be mainly pyrite. The streambed that receives the water that flows from the mine is also a dark red, which is also indicative of sulfide mineralization. Just east of the mine are former foundations and a large steel cylinder that was used in processing the mined material. Since this is a state park, collecting is not allowed, but it is still worth a visit to this mine as the dumps contain a lot of sulfides and the mine is in an incredibly scenic area.

References: Alling, 1917

41. Ironville Blue and Green Slag

Light blue glassy slag is relatively easy to find at this slag dump.

(See map on page 120.)
County: Essex
Site type: Slag dump
Land status: Private, posted against dumping, but parking area is along public road
Material: Glassy blue and green slag
Host rock: Slag
Difficulty: Easy
Family-friendly: Yes
Tools needed: Hammer
Special concerns: Uncertain of collecting status
Special attractions: Penfield Homestead Museum in nearby Ironville
GPS parking: N43° 55' 39" / W73° 35' 29"
GPS slag dump: N43° 55' 39" / W73° 35' 24"
Topographic quadrangle: Eagle Lake, NY
Finding the site: This site can be a tricky to find. It is located approximately 3.3 miles west of Ironville, and is not near the center of this former ironworks town.

The slag pile is easy to find once you are at the parking area.

From I-87, take exit 28 for NY 74 E. Proceed about 5.9 miles, and turn left on Letsonville Road. Continue 2.2 miles and Letsonville Road becomes Old Furnace Road. Proceed about 3.5 miles and look for a clearing and wide parking area to the left. There are some large piles of rock and dirt and at least one sign saying that dumping is prohibited. The slag pile forms the large bank of the hillside in the woods, and also extends to the south side of Old Furnace Road.

Rockhounding

This interesting site not only has glassy blue and green slag, but it is significant in terms of industrial history. The iron mines, which were mainly magnetite in gneissic rocks, were located to the southeast in Hammondville and were operated from the early 1800s to about 1893. The Hammondville area has numerous mines, as indicated on the Eagle Lake, NY topographic quadrangle, but unfortunately this area is private land and not accessible without permission. The ores were brought to the Penfield Iron Works in Ironville for separation, and were then shipped by rail to Lake Champlain. Separation of the ores by screening with water and gravity was very inefficient until the introduction of an industrial magnet that used electricity, an invention of Joseph Henry that was, in fact, the first industrial use of electricity. Thomas Davenport visited the Penfield Iron Works in 1833 and was quite intrigued by the magnet. At great expense, he bought one of these magnets and studied it intensely. He later used the principles he learned to develop the first electric motor. For this reason, the Penfield Iron Works at Penfield is often considered to be the birthplace of the electric motor and the industrial use of electricity.

A blast furnace was built in 1845 and produced pig iron. This furnace must have been located along Old Furnace Road and near Furnace Mountain and the Hammondville magnetite mines, given the location of the slag pile and the names of the road and the mountain. Once you are at the parking area, the slag is extremely easy to find. In addition to blue slag, the pile also has an abundance of glassy green, black, and white slag. The pieces are often solid frothy gray slag with a coating of glassy color. The glassy areas break with a conchoidal fracture pattern, and often show swirly bands of blue and green in a solid white background. This site is frequented by rockhounds as evidenced by the large amount of broken slag and pits in the bank. The pile was estimated to be approximately 50 feet wide and 20 feet high, and it extends into the woods for an unknown extent. Several pits have been dug in the woods by rock hunters who were undoubtedly looking for larger pieces of the colored slag.

If you get the opportunity, be sure to stop at the Penfield Homestead Museum. This museum, located at 703 Creek Rd., Crown Point, New York 12928 (near the center of Ironville just north of Penfield Pond) has a great deal of information on the local history and is a good resource for anyone interested in more of the history of the Penfield Iron Works and associated iron mines.

References: Newland, 1919; Penfield Foundation, 2013

42. Schroon Lake Roadcut Minerals

The coarse zones in the outcrop have distinct crystals of allanite, hornblende, and coarse potassium feldspar.

(See map on page 120.)

County: Warren

Site type: Roadcut

Land status: Uncertain, not posted, may be state land

Material: Allanite, hornblende, potassium feldspar

Host rock: Granitic gneiss

Difficulty: Moderate

Family-friendly: No, specialty minerals

Tools needed: Hammer, chisel

Special concerns: Road crossing, traffic

Special attractions: Schroon Lake

GPS parking: N43° 44' 43" / W73° 47' 58"

Topographic quadrangle: Chestertown, NY

The roadcuts are on the west side of Highway 9, and lots of parking is available on the east side of the road.

Finding the site: From I-87 heading north, take exit 26, and turn left (west) onto Valley Farm Road. Proceed 0.4 mile and turn right (northeast) onto US 9N. Continue 2.1 miles, and the parking area will be on the right. The outcrops are well exposed on the left side of the highway.

Rockhounding

The road cuts along US 9 near Schroon Lake expose gneissic rocks with some coarse pegmatitelike zones. At this roadcut you can see several dark minerals, which may be allanite and hornblende, surrounded by light-colored potassium feldspar and quartz. Breaking apart some of these rocks shows that the feldspar has excellent cleavage and some of the surfaces are perfectly flat and almost mirrorlike in their ability to reflect sunlight. Some other minerals that are reported in the cuts along US 9 at Schroon Lake are epidote, prehnite, datolite, and chabazite, but I did not see any of these minerals at this outcrop. The outcrops continue north for several thousand feet, but the stop referenced here had the best examples of minerals within the gneisses that I saw during my visit.

References: Robinson and Chamberlain, 2007

43. Minerva Railroad Cut Light Blue Calcite

Light blue calcite can be found in both outcrop and in loose rocks around the railroad tracks.

(See map on page 120.)

County: Essex

Site type: Outcrops along railroad

Land status: Vanderwhacker Mountain Wild Forest, rail line not posted

Material: Light blue calcite, tourmaline

Host rock: Coarse white marble surrounded by coarse gneisses

Difficulty: Easy

Family-friendly: Yes

Tools needed: Hammer, chisel

Special concerns: Bugs in summertime, railroad status subject to change.

Special attractions: Gore Mountain Ski Area and Lake George

GPS parking: N43° 49' 06" / W74° 03' 45"

GPS outcrops: N43° 49' 31" / W74° 04' 11"

Topographic quadrangle: Dutton Mountain, NY

The steep cliff sides offer some welcome shade on a hot summer day.

Finding the site: From I-87, take exit 26 to US 9N, and turn left onto Olmstedville Road, which is CR 29. Proceed about 6 miles to Olmstedville, and turn left (west) onto Main Street, then proceed about 1.7 miles and keep right (north) onto NY 28N. Go about 4.4 miles, and turn left onto North Woods Club Road. Proceed 4 miles, and park at the parking turnoff (which is very small) on the north side of the road next to the railroad tracks. Proceed north on the tracks for approximately 0.75 mile, and you will come to a steep cut with large boulders on both sides. The light blue calcite is in outcrops on the east side of the railroad cut.

Rockhounding

This is a great site, as it is very easy to find, and it is a relatively short and pleasant walk to the outcrops. For most rockhounds, the main mineral of interest here is the light blue calcite, but the gneissic rocks also have schorl tourmaline in some of the pegmatitic zones. The calcite occurs in large outcrops and is part of a large mass of recrystallized white marble. Graphite flakes are also common in the calcite. The light blue calcite crumbles easily, especially in the rocks that are coarse-grained calcite with minor graphite. In addition to these outcrops there is at least one more additional outcrop of calcite on the west side of the rail cut, approximately 0.5 mile from the parking area. The rail cut was originally built to serve the Tahawus titanium mine (site 44) and although it is currently not active, it is possible that the rail line may be opened again for shipping aggregate from the former Tahawus mine.

References: Zabriskie, 2006

44. Tahawus Mine Titaniferous Magnetite

This piece from the tailings is nearly entirely magnetite, and likely has some titanium as well.

(See map on page 120.)

County: Essex

Site type: Dumps of inactive mine

Land status: Private, not posted (former mine site)

Material: Titaniferous magnetite, labradorite

Host rock: Anorthosite, gabbro, gabbroic anorthosite

Difficulty: Easy

Family-friendly: Yes

Tools needed: Sledgehammer, hammer, chisel

Special concerns: Land status uncertain, highwalls near large lake

Special attractions: Headwaters of Hudson River

GPS parking: N44° 02' 38" / W74° 03' 27"

Topographic quadrangle: Santanoni Peak, NY

The western workings have filled with water and now form a huge lake that is surrounded with mine tailings.

Finding the site: From I-87, take exit 29 towards Newcomb. Turn left onto Blue Ridge Road, and continue for 13.2 miles, and the road becomes Boreas Road. Continue 3.1 miles. The road then becomes CR 84. Continue 1.1 miles until you reach the intersection with Tahawus Road. Tahawus Road is also shown on many maps as CR 25. The distance from exit 29 to Tahawus Road is approximately 17.4 miles. Turn right (north) on Tahawus Road, and proceed about 6.4 miles to the parking area at a sharp bend in the road. You can park here and hike over nonposted ground to the mine dumps, which are approximately 0.25 mile north and adjacent to the former open-pit mine, which is now a large lake.

Rockhounding

The Tahawus mine has a long history. In 1826, prospectors searching for silver discovered magnetite in the area. The site was subsequently developed into an iron mine, but it was so remote that transportation of the ore was a serious issue. Another problem was that the high percentage of ilmenite and sphene, which contain titanium, made ore processing difficult. However, US supplies of titanium were cut off during World War II, and the mine was reopened in 1941 by National Lead Company to produce this element. A rail line was built from North Creek to the mine (see site 43, Minerva Railroad Cut Light Blue Calcite). A huge complex to produce titanium dioxide and iron oxide was constructed at the mine, and mining and processing continued until 1989, when the last ore train left the mine. Nearly all of the former processing buildings were demolished in 2006.

This is an easy site to visit, but you must make sure to stay away from posted ground. During my first visit to this site, I came to the main gate at the end of the road, and it was clearly marked no trespassing. Other visitors were at the site and passing through the fence, but I decided against joining them, and went to the parking area on the other side of the hill. I was able to walk to the dumps on the southwest side of the lake formed from the former mine without passing any posted ground, and there were many footpaths and abundant trash, which indicated that people frequented this area. You can easily find large boulders with shiny magnetite and lots of anorthosite and gabbro.

The banks of the lake are often very steep and are loaded with magnetite and associated minerals.

I could not distinguish the ilmenite from the magnetite, and could not recognize the sphene, but found that the magnetite itself was quite interesting, as it is very abundant and extremely dense when compared to similar rocks without abundant magnetite. The highwalls of the former mine form extremely steep cliffs and slopes along the lake, so be extremely careful as you walk near the edges of the lake.

References: Jensen, 1978; Stephenson, 1945; Zabriskie, 2006

45. Blue Ridge Labradorite

The labradorite is found along the banks of the stream.

(See map on page 120.)
County: Essex
Site type: Boulders along stream
Land status: Fishing access point along stream
Material: Labradorite with schiller
Host rock: Boulders and cobbles are found as loose material.
Difficulty: Easy
Family-friendly: Yes, but must be careful of water
Tools needed: Sledgehammer, hammer
Special concerns: Streambanks overgrown, near water, some land possibly private
Special attractions: Fishing in nearby rivers and lakes
GPS parking: N43° 57' 23" / W73° 45' 50"
Topographic quadrangle: Blue Ridge, NY
Finding the site: Take I-87 to exit 29, and turn left (west) onto Blue Ridge Road (CR 2b). Proceed 1.6 miles, and look for a parking area on the left (south). The labradorite is found as small boulders and cobbles along the bank of the stream.

Fresh pieces of labradorite, when wet and reflected in the sun, often show good schiller.

Rockhounding

Fortunately, you do not need to get wet at this site. The best labradorite is found on the banks as rounded gray rocks that range from a few inches to a foot in diameter. The pieces with the best schiller are the coarsest pieces, and you may have to break a cobble into pieces to expose fresh labradorite. The schiller is best seen in bright sunlight. If it is cloudy, you will likely not be able to see it. These rocks are extremely hard and difficult to break, especially as they are often rounded and the hammer cannot easily strike a flat surface. A sledgehammer may be useful for some of the larger rocks. Pieces can generally be found by brushing away pine needles, digging into the ground, and looking for protrusions of gray labradorite through the soil. In addition to this location, there may be other locations up- and downstream that may have similar rocks.

References: Zabriskie, 2006

46. Newcomb Highway 28 Calcite with Graphite

The eastern roadcut is very small and easy to miss, but has a lot of loose light orange calcite.

(See map on page 120.)
County: Essex
Site type: Roadcut
Land status: Likely in highway right-of-way, not posted
Material: Light orange calcite with minor graphite in eastern roadcut, white calcite with graphite in western roadcut.
Host rock: Marble
Difficulty: Easy
Family-friendly: Yes, but best for a brief visit only due to traffic
Tools needed: Hammer, chisel
Special concerns: Traffic on highway, must be careful to pull off safely
Special attractions: Long Lake
GPS parking, eastern roadcut: N43° 58' 06" / W74° 10' 14"
GPS parking, western roadcut: N43° 58' 18" / W74°10' 51"

Topographic quadrangle: Newcomb, NY

Finding the site: From I-87, take exit 29 towards Newcomb. Turn left onto Blue Ridge Road, and continue for 13.2 miles, and the road becomes Boreas Road. Continue 3.1 miles. The road then becomes CR 84. Continue 1.1 miles until you reach the intersection with Tahawus Road (CR 25), and stay to the left. Continue 1.3 miles to the intersection with NY 28N, turn right (west), and proceed 5.2 miles to the first roadcut. This eastern roadcut is best described as a small, sloping bank with loose calcite, and it is very easy to miss if you are not looking at the roadside closely. The western roadcut is approximately 0.6 mile west, just south of Belden Lake, and consists of walls of calcite that line both sides of the road.

Rockhounding

This calcite at the eastern roadcut has a very slight orange tint from iron-bearing minerals. The roadcut has an abundance of loose calcite, and many of these pieces are fist size, coarse grained, and contain small blebs of graphite. Most of the calcite at the eastern roadcut shows excellent cleavage and breaks apart easily when tapped with a hammer. The western roadcut is much larger and has large exposures of calcite on both sides of the highway. The calcite is much whiter in this area, but blebs of graphite are common throughout the rock. Despite the size of the western road-cut, there are not many loose rocks on the ground, and the vertical walls are generally very intact and hard. There is also a lot of vegetation on the sides of the road. You will have to be careful to avoid poison ivy and ticks if you take a close look at this area, but you are guaranteed to see some excellent calcite with graphite on the roadcut walls.

References: Zabriskie, 2006

This calcite from the eastern roadcut has small dark blebs of graphite.

47. Long Lake Highway 30 Fluorite and Calcite

Fluorite and calcite can be seen in veins in the gneissic rocks.

(See map on page 120.)

County: Hamilton

Site type: Roadcut

Land status: Uncertain, not posted

Material: Fluorite and calcite

Host rock: Granitic gneiss

Difficulty: Moderate

Family-friendly: No, outcrops relatively small, specialty minerals only

Tools needed: Hammer, chisel

Special concerns: Must cross NY 30, drainage ditch often wet

Special attractions: Long Lake

GPS parking: N44° 03' 02" / W74° 31' 20"

Topographic quadrangle: Little Tupper Lake, NY

Finding the site: From I-87, take exit 29 towards Newcomb. Turn left onto Blue Ridge Road, and continue for 13.2 miles, and the road becomes Boreas Road.

The roadcut is on the west side of Highway 30 opposite the parking area at Moonshine Pond Road.

Continue 3.1 miles. The road then becomes CR 84. Continue 1.1 miles until you reach the intersection with CR 25, also called Tahawus Road. Continue another 1.3 miles to the intersection with NY 28N, and head west for another 18.6 miles. At the small town of Long Lake, turn right (north) onto NY 30. Continue 7.9 miles, and park on the right (east) side of the road at the intersection of Moonshine Pond Road and NY 30. Be sure to park well off the highway as NY 30 gets quite a bit of traffic.

Rockhounding

This site is reportedly north of a roadcut that was heavily collected between 1994 and 1995. The bulk of the collectable minerals was removed, and the outcrops were then seeded and tarred over. The location that was covered was reported to be at N44° 02' 42" / W74° 31' 16", which is the next set of outcrops south of this site. I originally tried to reach this area, but I was not able to find a safe parking place for access. Instead I parked at the nearest parking place, which was approximately 0.25 mile farther north on NY 30, and went to the roadcuts across from the parking area near Moonshine Pond Road. I reasoned that the geology would be similar in this area.

A fairly large vein with fluorite and calcite, which is approximately 6 inches wide, is well exposed at this outcrop, and there are several black and tan minerals that I could not identify in nearby veins in the gneiss. Unfortunately, I was unable to check out the outcrops farther to the south, but they may still be worth evaluating even though the mineralized areas are reported to have been covered.

References: Richards and Robinson, 2000; Robinson and Chamberlain, 2007

48. Roaring Brook Falls Labradorite

This is a typical boulder of labradorite that is found at the base of Roaring Brook Falls.

County: Essex
Site type: Rocks at base of waterfall
Land status: Giant Mountain Wilderness Area
Material: Labradorite
Host rock: Precambrian meta-anorthosite gneiss
Difficulty: Easy
Family-friendly: Yes
Tools needed: None
Special concerns: Some hiking, slippery rocks
Special attractions: Giant Mountain Wilderness and other nearby areas
GPS parking: N44° 09' 01" / W 73° 46' 03"
GPS base of falls: N44° 09' 01" / W73° 45' 39"
Topographic quadrangle: Keene Valley, NY
Finding the site: From I-87, take exit 30 for US 9 towards NY 73. Go 0.2 mile, and turn left (northwest) on US 9N. Continue 2.2 miles, and stay left towards NY 73. Go

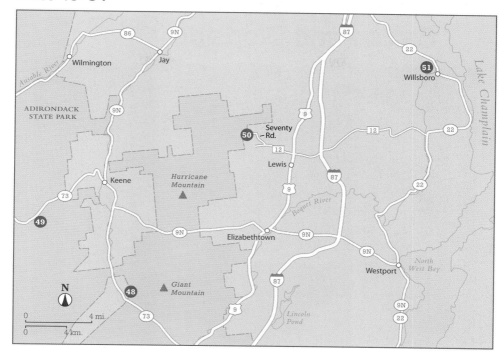

5.3 miles on NY 73, and you will see a parking area on the right. This area gets very crowded. Park here, and walk east on the trail to Roaring Brook Falls.

Rockhounding

This is an easy site in which to find labradorite rocks in a wide variety of sizes, from small stones to huge boulders. The labradorite is found in outcrop and all around the base of the falls. Not all of it exhibits a schiller, and sometimes you have to break apart a piece to see the play in colors. The schiller, when it is present, is best seen in bright sunlight. The area around the falls is heavily forested, and depending on the weather it may be difficult to get good sunlight when you are looking at the rocks. The rocks around the waterfall can be slippery, and during high water, the falls undoubtedly become much larger. In addition, since this is part of the Giant Mountain Wilderness area, rock collecting is technically not allowed, but you are certainly still able to hike to this area and look at the rocks.

References: Zabriskie, 2006

49. Cascade Lakes Calcite and Diopside

This rounded piece of green diopside and calcite was found in the stream.

(See map on page 141.)

County: Essex

Site type: Stream valley below waterfall

Land status: Adirondack Forest Preserve, Cascade Lakes day-use area

Material: Calcite, diopside, garnet, labradorite

Host rock: Metanorthosite, gneiss, marble

Difficulty: Easy

Family-friendly: Yes

Tools needed: Hammer, chisel

Special concerns: Steep hike towards waterfall, slippery rocks in stream

Special attractions: Cascade Lakes

GPS parking: N44° 13' 32" / W73° 52' 29"

Topographic quadrangle: Keene Valley, NY

Finding the site: From I-87, take exit 30 for US 9 to NY 73 towards Keene. Once on US 9, proceed 2.2 miles to NY 73, and turn slightly left (west). Continue on NY 73 for

The falls are easy to see from the highway and provide a great setting for your visit.

approximately 19 miles. You will see two large lakes, which are the Lower and Upper Cascade Lakes, and a waterfall coming off the mountainside between the lakes. This area can be very congested with car traffic and bicyclists, especially during the summer and weekends. The turnoff is a very sharp left, so drive past this area, make a U-turn when you can (which may take a few miles) and come back and take the entrance drive on the right (south) side of NY 73 to the parking area. This is a day-use area and has a restroom and picnic tables. Hike between the lakes and up the trails to the stream below the waterfall; the rocks are found throughout this stream.

Rockhounding

This is great site for anyone visiting the Adirondacks, as it has a very nice day-use area and offers a great view of an Adirondack waterfall descending the appropriately named Cascade Mountain. The stream has an abundant and continuously replenished supply of rocks from the upper reaches of the mountain. Blue calcite, white calcite, calcite with green and brown diopside, brown garnet, and labradorite, some of which has minor schiller, can easily be found in the rocks of the streambed. The area is frequented by rockhounds, as fragments of calcite, garnet, and diopside are commonly found on top of boulders and other areas where they would not occur naturally. The trail to the stream and the falls is not well maintained and is subject to occasional washouts, so be extremely careful when hiking up the stream valley towards the waterfall.

References: Zabriskie, 2006; Robinson and Chamberlain, 2007

50. Lewis Mine Entrance Wollastonite

This wollastonite piece, studded with garnet, was found on the ground outside the mine gates.

(See map on page 141.)

County: Essex

Site type: Waste rocks at mine entrance

Land status: Private, but next to public road

Material: Wollastonite, garnet, diopside

Host rock: Skarn at Lewis Mine

Difficulty: Extremely easy

Family-friendly: Yes

Tools needed: Hammer, chisel

Special concerns: Limited collecting. Do not go when trucks are actively entering site.

Special attractions: None

GPS parking: N44° 18' 05" / W73° 36' 34"

Topographic quadrangle: Lewis, NY

They are not much to look at, but the drainages and piles outside of the mine gates often have wollastonite with garnet and diopside.

Finding the site: From I-87, take exit 32 towards Lewis. Turn left on Stowersville Road, go 1.7 miles, then continue on Wells Hill Road for 2 miles. Take a slight right onto Seventy Road, go 0.4 mile, and then take a sharp right (north) to stay on Seventy Road. Go 0.5 mile, and park on the west side of the road before the mine entrance. The minerals are found as waste rocks scattered outside of the gate.

Rockhounding

This is the gate outside of an active wollastonite mine, often referred to as the Lewis mine, as Lewis is the nearest town. It would be great to get to go to the actual mine, but if you cannot get permission, the next best option is to get some of the rocks that may have fallen off the trucks or found their way outside some other way. The drainages on both sides of the road had some very nice pieces of fibrous wollastonite, reddish brown garnet, and dark green diopside when I was at this site in late June 2013. It was on a Saturday afternoon, and the mine was closed, so it was not a problem to look for rocks outside the gate. However, if you do visit this on a weekday or other day that the mine is open, make sure that you do not cause any problems with mine activities.

References: Zabriskie, 2006

51. Willsboro Dump Road Wollastonite, Garnet, and Diopside

This pile on Dump Road, while very small, is full rocks with wollastonite, garnet, and diopside.

(See map on page 141.)

County: Essex

Site type: Small pile of mineralized rocks

Land status: Next to public road and adjacent to private property

Material: Wollastonite, garnet, and diopside

Host rock: Skarn deposit (mined from the Lewis mine to the west)

Difficulty: Extremely easy

Family-friendly: Yes, but only for a brief visit to look at minerals

Tools needed: None

Special concerns: Next to active mineral-processing plant and private land

Special attractions: Ausable Chasm, Lake Champlain

GPS parking: N44° 21' 37" / W73° 24' 26"

Topographic quadrangle: Willsboro, NY-VT

Finding the site: From I-87, take exit 33 towards NY 22S, and continue on NY 22 for 8.2 miles. Turn right on South Mountain View Drive, go 0.8 mile, and take the third right onto Dump Road. Dump Road is just past the large mineral processing facility. Go about 0.2 mile and you will see a private road to the right, which leads to the northern end of the processing complex. The small rock pile is just below the plant processing sign at the corner of this private dump road.

This piece of wollastonite with garnet and diopside was found on this pile of rock next to the road.

Rockhounding

This is a very, very small site, and it would normally never be included in a guidebook like this except for the incredible quality of the minerals in this limited area. The rocks are from a wollastonite mine located near Lewis, and they are brought to this Willsboro plant for processing. Around mineral-processing plants like this, you can often find interesting minerals along nearby public roads. This site is no exception. The pile is apparently the result of rocks that have either fallen out of trucks or simply washed down the road, but it is uncertain how often the site is replenished with new waste rocks. At first glance it looks like just an ordinary pile, but it is full of white to light green wollastonite that is embedded with brown garnet and dark green diopside. You can literally step out of your car and find pieces that could be in a museum. You do not even need a hammer, as most of the pieces are already reduced to hand sample size. The mine itself must produce tremendous mineral specimens. Many of the wollastonite crystals are elongated and have a fiberlike character, but they are also relatively hard, and the rocks are difficult to break apart. If you visit this site, bear in mind that while this is a public road, the rocks are from an active wollastonite processing plant. Stay away from the fenced areas and truck traffic, and keep your visit brief so you do not disrupt any work being done. Since the site is so small, you should be very reasonable with the amount of rocks that you collect from this site, and be sure to leave some good pieces for future rockhounds.

References: Herod, 1984

52. Lyon Mountain Magnetite

The Lyon Mountain magnetite ores were remarkably pure and rich in iron.

County: Clinton
Site type: Mine dump
Land status: Owned by town of Dannemora
Material: Magnetite
Host rock: Granitic gneiss
Difficulty: Easy
Family-friendly: Yes
Tools needed: Sledgehammer, hammer, chisel
Special concerns: Some deep inclined mine shafts near trail, requires some hiking
Special attractions: Lyon Mountain Mining and Railroad Museum
GPS parking: N44° 43' 06" / W73° 54' 37"
GPS magnetite dump: N44° 43' 03" / W73° 54' 29"
Topographic quadrangle: Lyon Mountain, NY
Finding the site: This can be a difficult site to find, as it is in the woods and cannot be seen from the road. From I-87, take exit 37, and turn left onto NY 3W, go 1 mile,

Sites 52–53

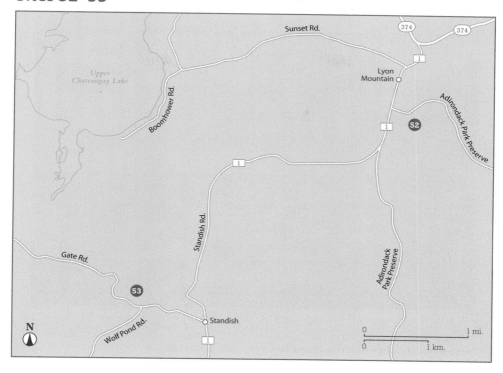

and turn right onto NY 190W (Military Turnpike), and go northwest about 1.8 miles. Turn left (west) onto NY 374W, and proceed approximately 22 miles to Lyon Mountain. Take the left fork (southwest) onto Saranac Street, and continue about 1,000 feet and turn left (south) onto 1st Street, which becomes Standish Road. First Street is also referred to as CR 1 on Google Maps. Go about 4,000 feet and turn left (east) onto Power House Road. Go about 0.2 mile, and turn right (south) on Petes Street. Proceed 0.1 mile to the end of the road and a gate (which is not posted), and park here. Be sure that you are not blocking the gate. Walk through a small circular gravel area to the south, and follow a very indistinct footpath through the woods. You will emerge at a small road that is used by ATVs. Turn right (west) and walk until this road intersects with another ATV road. This road turns sharply to the left (east). Follow this road until you reach the mine dump. On the way you will see some steep slopes and shafts to the left (north) and at least one mine adit to the right (south). The principal mine dump is a bank that is full of magnetite in granitic gneiss, and it is located in the middle of a broad, tree-filled cut through the mountainside.

The magnetite mine dump forms a prominent wall in the broad trench.

Rockhounding

The Lyon Mountain deposits were discovered in the early 1800s, and the deposits were first worked in the 1860s. Several iron deposits were being discovered and worked throughout New York and elsewhere in the country, and the rocks at Lyon Mountain were recognized for their rich magnetite ore. Rail service was extended to Lyon Mountain in 1879, and the Chateaugay Ore & Iron Company was organized. For many years the west side of the mine was worked by open cuts and inclined shafts to a depth of about 900 feet, and the mines extended along the strike of the magnetite bodies for about 2,000 feet. Around 1920 the mine came under new management, which implemented more modern mining methods. After the west side ores were nearly depleted, production centered on underground workings on the east side. The mines became some of the deepest commercial iron mines in the United States, with stopes as much as 3,500 feet below the surface. The ore was low in phosphorous, and was considered some of the best in the industry. It was used in the construction of the Brooklyn, George Washington, and Golden Gate Bridges, and production was dramatically ramped up during World War II and the early years of the Cold War. Republic Steel took over the mines in 1939, but the expense of underground mining combined with depletion of the near-surface ores ultimately resulted in the mines no longer being economically productive. The mines closed for good in 1967, throwing virtually the entire town out of work. Like most mining towns, Lyon Mountain had a violent and often disturbing history. Many men were killed in the mines, and many others were killed in above-ground fights and other violence brought on by strikes, crime, poverty, and the incredible stress of working in a deep underground iron mine.

I was very lucky during my visit to the area, as I was escorted by a local who showed me the magnetite mine dump in the broad mine cuts on the eastern side of the mountain. He said the area was often used by ATV riders. We were able to reach this area without crossing any land that was posted against trespassing. The magnetite on the dump is very striking in its density and apparent purity. Many pieces are nearly solid black metallic magnetite and have bands of orange feldspar and clear-to-white quartz. Some also have small cavities in which octahedral crystals of magnetite can be seen. The Lyon Mountain area also has some very large sand tailings, which are better described as small mountains as opposed to piles, but these are nearly devoid of rocks. Some of the former mine buildings are also still standing, but these are located well north of the trenches and magnetite dump. There is also a huge slag pile from the furnace that processed the ores in nearby Standish (Site 53).

If you get the opportunity, you may also want to visit The Lyon Mountain Mining and Railroad Museum, which is housed in the former Delaware and Hudson Railroad Station on Standish Road in Lyon Mountain. Its website gives information on hours and days open to the public.

References: Newland, 1919; Gallagher, 1937; Gooley, 2004, 2005

53. Standish Slag

Many pieces of Standish Slag have a pungent sulfur smell and rounded blobs of iron in their interiors.

(See map on page 149.)

County: Clinton and Franklin

Site type: Slag pile

Land status: Private and state land

Material: Slag

Host rock: Slag processed from Lyon Mountain iron mines

Difficulty: Easy

Family-friendly: No, but maybe for adventurous families

Tools needed: Hammer

Special concerns: Unstable slopes, stream crossing

Special attractions: Nearby iron mine north of Standish

GPS parking: N44° 41' 29" / W73° 57' 43"

GPS west end of slag pile: N44° 41' 36" / W73° 57' 52"

GPS parking for road to nearby iron mine: N44° 42' 31" / W73° 56' 55"

GPS nearby iron mine: N44° 42' 15" / W73° 56' 42"

Topographic quadrangle: Lyon Mountain, NY

Only the hardiest plants can grow on the slag, and it is rapidly eroding and washing into Standish Creek.

Finding the site: From I-87, take exit 37, turn left onto NY 3W, go 1 mile, and turn right onto NY 190W (Military Turnpike), and go about 1.8 miles. Turn left onto NY 374W, and proceed about 22 miles to Lyon Mountain. Take the left fork (southwest) onto Saranac Street, and continue about 1,000 feet and turn left (south) onto 1st Street, which becomes Standish Road. First Street is also referred to as CR 1 on Google Maps. Continue on Standish Road for about 3.8 miles. In Standish, turn right onto Wolf Pond Road, and follow this southwest and then west for 0.4 mile to Gate Road. This is a gate for state land, and the boundary starts at the Clinton/Franklin County boundary. Walk past the gate, and you will soon be able to see the slag pile through the woods, which is across Standish Brook. Unfortunately, there are no trails to reach the brook, so you have to bushwhack downslope, walk across the brook, and then you are at the base of the slag pile. This western end of the slag pile is state land, while the eastern half is private, but there are no signs indicating where the private property starts once you get on the pile. There is another gate to the north on the west end of Standish, but this is posted against trespassing.

Rockhounding

This is reportedly the largest of the slag piles left in the Adirondacks. The slag is from the blast furnace that operated at Standish from the late 1800s to about 1935. The blast furnace processed the high-quality iron ores that came from the Lyon Mountain iron mines. The pile is huge—nearly 60 feet high in some places. It covers more than 5 acres, based on a review of satellite photos.

The slag is mostly gray and glassy, and it is weathering fairly quickly. Unfortunately, as it breaks down it also enters Standish Creek, which is certainly not good for the creek. Some of the pieces are a glassy blue gray, some are highly vesicular, and some have spherical balls of iron-rich globules that did not get assimilated into the glassy matrix of the slag. Many of these pieces have an incredibly strong smell of sulfur when broken open. The pile was also used for disposal of debris, as many large pieces of rusty, twisted steel and iron protrude from parts of the pile. The slopes of some of the larger piles are extremely unstable, and should be avoided. However, once you get into the main parts of the pile the area is very flat, and somewhat resembles a lunar landscape with depressions, small hills, and general lack of vegetation. Incredibly, some plants do grow on the slag, but many parts are nearly free of any plant or animal life even after nearly eighty years of inactivity. This site is worth exploring, but it is only for the most adventurous of rockhounds. Be sure to bring good boots and gloves, as you will get wet and have to climb and cross some difficult terrain.

As an added bonus, the topographic map for the area indicates that a former iron mine is located north of Standish. The coordinates are given in the first part of this entry. I stopped by the entrance road briefly, and noted that the area is completely undeveloped and did not have any "no trespassing" signs. If this area is accessible, it is only a short walk from Standish Road, and may be worth exploring. I did not get to visit this mine, as by then it was too dark to go, but I will certainly try to go to this mine the next time I am in the Standish/Lyon Mountain area.

References: Farthing and Sidlaukas, 2006

54. Pierrepont Dillabough Road Hematite

This specular hematite was found just off the south side of Dillabough Road.

County: St. Lawrence
Site type: Loose rocks along roadside
Land status: State forest and private land
Material: Hematite (specular and earthy) and limonite
Host rock: Potsdam Sandstone
Difficulty: Easy
Family-friendly: Yes
Tools needed: Hammer
Special concerns: Will likely get muddy, limited parking
Special attractions: Higley Flow State Park
GPS parking at gate: N44° 30' 33" / W75° 01' 24"
GPS parking on road: N44° 30' 48" / W75° 01' 04"
Topographic quadrangle: Pierrepont, NY
Finding the site: From Canton, take NY 68E southeast for 7.9 miles, and turn right (southwest) onto CR 24, which is Clare Town Line-Pierrepont Center Road. Go 2.1

Sites 54–66

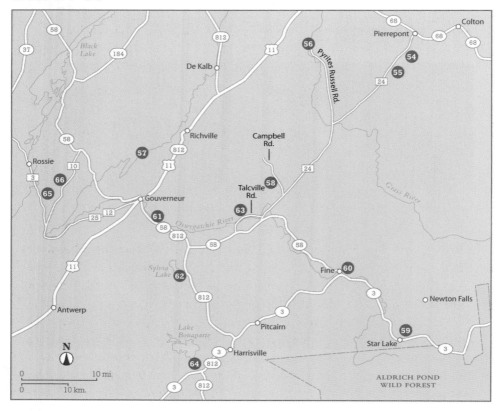

miles and turn left (south) onto Crary Road, and go 0.5 mile. Turn left onto Dillabough Road, go 0.2 mile, where a parking area is on the right (south) just west of a gate. This gate is unlocked, but the road is very narrow and if wet may be difficult for your vehicle. I opted to take the road and parked at the coordinates listed above. However, it turns out the hematitic rocks are found along the south side of Dillabough Road, so you may as well walk and look for the rocks. Be aware that your GPS may suggest that you reach the site via the northern end of Dillabough Road. I do not recommend this, as Google Maps indicate that this road does not exist. This usually means it is a road that has degenerated into a trail, and no longer supports travel by vehicle.

Rockhounding

This is an unusual site in that it is along a road, but there are no outcrops. The site has fragments of hematitic breccias of the Late Cambrian-Early Ordovician

The hematitic rocks can be found in the shallow drainage on the south side of Dillabough Road.

Potsdam Sandstone, and these can be found along the south side of Dillabough Road. Simply look for large, red muddy rocks, and break them open. Many of them have bright red hematite, zones of orange limonite, and quartz. Some of the hematite is specular, but these pieces appeared to be relatively rare. It is possible that there are some mines or prospect pits in the area that provide good outcrops and exposures of these rocks, but I was not able to locate them. There are also many other rocks in the area, and not all of them contain hematite. I also hiked upslope into the woods, but did not find any hematitic rocks. The best pieces appeared to be on the roadside. This actually makes the site a good site to bring others, as it is a pleasant walk along the road, and it is relatively easy to spot the hematite. If you get lucky you may find some good specular hematite. Please also note that the area north of Dillabough Road, which is a swamp, is private land, and other private, posted land is also along the road.

References: Buddington and Leonard, 1962; Robinson and Chamberlain, 2007

This is a typical example of the hematite-limonite breccia formed in the Potsdam Sandstone along Dillabough Road.

55. West Pierrepont Selleck Road Tremolite

This piece had some green tremolite and I suspect that the black mineral may be uvite, but I could not tell for certain.

(See map on page 156.)

County: St. Lawrence
Site type: Outcrops developed by small workings
Land status: Taylor Creek State Forest
Material: Tremolite
Host rock: Metasedimentary gneiss
Difficulty: Easy
Family-friendly: Yes
Tools needed: Sledgehammer, hammer, chisel
Special concerns: Unpaved road to the site
Special attractions: None
GPS parking: N44° 29' 28" / W75° 02' 19"
Topographic quadrangle: West Pierrepont, NY

The workings are in the woods about 200 feet west of the parking area.

Finding the site: From I-81, take exit 48 to I-781/Fort Drum Connector, continue about 4.3 miles, then take exit 4 to US 11. Continue 51.6 miles north to Canton, and turn right (east) onto Main Street. Take the second right (southeast) to CR 27/Park Street. Continue 7.2 miles, turn left (east) on Allen Road, continue 0.6 mile and turn right (south) onto Plains Road. Go 1.9 miles and turn left (northeast) onto CR 24/Claire Town Line-Pierrepont Center Road. Go 0.1 mile and turn right (east) onto Selleck Road. Go 1.1 miles, and look for an obscure turnoff to the right (south). Park at the crest of a small east-west trending broad ridge, walk west approximately 200 feet, and you will see the workings.

Rockhounding

This is an interesting site, as the rocks are well exposed in a small group of trenches that have been worked by previous rockhounds. Some of the tremolite is green and gemmy, and forms aggregates of crystals. Uvite, phlogopite, and orange calcite can also be found in the rocks. The small workings referenced here are approximately 200 feet west of the parking area, which is right next to the entrance road. An additional area for collecting is reportedly several hundred yards east of the parking area at the western base of the first east–west ridge, so it may also be worth exploring along the ridge to identify other workings and mineralized rocks.

References: Robinson and Chamberlain, 2007; Chamberlain et al., 2011

56. Pyrites Pyrite

The pyrite-bearing outcrops can easily be seen from the Grass River Bridge, and are on the east bank of the river.

(See map on page 156.)

County: St. Lawrence

Site type: Outcrop east bank of Grass River

Land status: Uncertain, not posted, reportedly accessible to public

Material: Pyrite and associated minerals

Host rock: Precambrian gneiss, gabbro, and amphibolite

Difficulty: Easy

Family-friendly: Yes

Tools needed: Sledgehammer, hammer, chisel

Special concerns: Area possibly difficult to access during high water

Special attractions: None

GPS parking: N44° 31' 25" / W75° 11' 31"

GPS outcrops: N44° 31' 24" /W75° 11' 27"

Topographic quadrangle: Canton, NY

Finding the site: From Canton, take US 11 south for 5 miles. Turn left (southeast) onto Eddy-Pyrites Road, and go 2.4 miles. Turn left on CR 21, which is Hermon-Pyrites Road, and go 0.2 mile. As you approach the bridge that crosses the Grass River, you can see the orange outcrops of the site on the east bank of the river south of the bridge. The sign on the bridge says Grasse River, but many maps reference it as Grass River. A parking area is on the north side on the road just after you cross the Grass River. A well-established trail is in the woods on the south side of the road. Follow this trail about 300 feet to the site, which is on the east bank of the Grass River.

Rockhounding

This is one of numerous pyrite belts in Precambrian gneisses in St. Lawrence and Jefferson Counties, and it is one of the few that I know of that can be easily accessed. The site was first worked for sulfur and iron around 1886. An attempt to open the mine occurred around 1905 to 1906, with the last work around 1907. Approximately 900 tons of crude ore were extracted, but work ceased shortly afterwards. Processing pyrite for iron and sulfur can be very messy and expensive, and this almost certainly soon made the site unprofitable. As of 2013 the only indications of mining at the site are the former adit just east of the river, at least from what I could see.

The trail from the road leads right to the outcrops on the east bank of the Grass River. Much of the rock is heavily stained with limonite and appears to have some hydrothermal alteration. The outcrop reportedly also has a 2-meter-wide undeformed phlogopite lamprophyre dike that cuts across the complex, but I did not see this dike during my site visit. Small areas of pyrite can be found in the gneisses and throughout much of the outcrop, but many of these are well within the harder sections of the outcrop. The easily obtainable pieces were undoubtedly chipped away by previous miners and rockhounds long ago, but with a little effort you should be able to find some interesting examples of pyrite. Recent research by the New York Geological Survey indicates that this outcrop is part of a section of oceanic crust and upper-mantle material that was pushed on top of the continent and later combined with supracrustal metasediments, and this offers new insights into the Precambrian geology of the region and the origin of this part of the Adirondacks.

Unaltered pyrite can easily be seen in the outcrops but the easy-to-get pieces have long been removed by previous rockhounds.

References: Buddington, 1917; Chiarenzelli et al., 2011

57. Richville Rock Island Roadcut Calcite

These clear calcite crystals were found in rubble along the base of the roadcut.

(See map on page 156.)
County: St. Lawrence
Site type: Roadcut
Land status: Private, not posted
Material: Calcite
Host rock: Coarse marble
Difficulty: Easy
Family-friendly: Yes
Tools needed: Hammer, chisel
Special concerns: Traffic on roadway, highwalls along roadcut
Special attractions: None
GPS parking: N44° 23' 41" / W75° 27' 13"
Topographic quadrangle: Richville, NY

The roadcut is mainly coarse marble, and some fractured zones have calcite crystals.

Finding the site: From I-81, take exit 48 to I-781/Fort Drum Connector, continue about 4.3 miles, and take exit 4 to US 11. Proceed on US 11 for about 34.2 miles to the town of Governeur, and turn left (north) on Rock Island Street, which turns into CR 11. Proceed about 3.6 miles to the junction with the Oswegatchie River. Make a U-turn, and park in a small area on the right (west) side of the road. The outcrops line both sides of the road south of the parking area.

Rockhounding

This long, well-exposed roadcut is mainly coarse marble. Calcite crystals can be found in some sheared and faulted zones, and potential areas have been dug out by previous rockhounds. You may be able to find some crystals on the walls and in the rubble at the base of the roadcuts. This site also has some large gray boulders that appear to be mainly tremolite and wollastonite. These were likely placed in this area to stabilize part of the roadside. Previous collectors have exposed some fresh surfaces in these boulders, revealing snow-white interiors and bladed crystals of wollastonite. The calcite crystals and wollastonite make this an excellent stop when in the area.

References: Robinson and Chamberlain, 2007

58. Edwards Campbell Road Calcite

This aggregate of calcite crystals was found on the ground in the loose rocks near the roadcut.

(See map on page 156.)
County: St. Lawrence
Site type: Roadcut
Land status: Trout Lake State Forest
Material: Calcite
Host rock: Recrystallized limestone
Difficulty: Easy
Family-friendly: Yes
Tools needed: Hammer, chisel
Special concerns: Traffic on roadside
Special attractions: None
GPS parking: N44° 21' 27" / W75° 14' 22"
Topographic quadrangle: South Edwards, NY

The road cut is easy to find and parking is adequate for your vehicle.

Finding the site: From I-81, take exit 48 to I-781/Fort Drum Connector, continue about 4.3 miles, and take exit 4 to US 11. Proceed on US 11 for about 34 miles to the town of Gouverneur, and turn right (south) on NY 58. Continue 14.2 miles and turn left (north) onto Maple Avenue Spur, continue 0.8 mile, and turn right (east) onto CR 24/Main Street. Go 1.5 miles, and turn left (north) onto Campbell Road. The road cut is approximately 1.3 miles farther and on the left (west) side of Campbell Road.

Rockhounding

This roadcut is located approximately 2 miles northeast of the former zinc mine at Edwards, which unfortunately is posted and no longer accessible without permission. The roadcut is near an area called the "Dodge Ore Bed," which reportedly contained hematite and quartz as well as calcite. This road-cut is a well-exposed mass of recrystallized limestone that has an abundance of coarse calcite with good cleavage and small rhombohedral crystals. The outcrop is frequented by rockhounds as there are several broken rocks on the outcrop. While quartz and hematite are reported in the area, I could not find any significant hematite mineralization or quartz crystals, but the abundance of calcite make this a worthwhile site to visit. Parking is excellent at this location and you should have no problem finding some interesting calcite.

References: Robinson and Chamberlain, 2007

59. Star Lake Benson Mines Minerals

This is an extensive waste rock pile with abundant sulfides, magnetite, and other minerals.

(See map on page 156.)
County: St. Lawrence
Site type: Waste rock piles at former iron mine
Land status: Private, but not posted at access area
Material: Sulfides, magnetite, garnet, sillimanite
Host rock: Metasedimentary gneisses
Difficulty: Easy
Family-friendly: Yes, but must be aware of potential access/land status changes
Tools needed: Sledgehammer, hammer, chisel
Special concerns: Land status uncertain, access may change
Special attractions: None
GPS parking: N44° 10' 01" / W75° 00' 52"
GPS rock piles: N44° 10' 01" / W75° 00' 18"
Topographic quadrangle: Oswegatchie, NY
Finding the site: From I-81, take exit 44 to Watertown, and go through the town until you reach NY 3E. Continue on NY 3E for approximately 54.6 miles to the hamlet of Star Lake, and turn left on Star Lake Road. Proceed about 0.4 mile,

and turn left onto Benson Mines Golf Course Road. Go about 320 feet to the intersection with Larose Road and the railroad tracks, and park on the south side of the tracks on the east side of Larose Road. You can then walk down the inactive rail line to the Benson Mines area. This route is not posted against trespassing, but be aware that land status and signs can change at any time.

Rockhounding

The Benson Mines were first identified as a potential iron deposit in 1810, when engineers noticed that their compasses did not function correctly in the area. However, it was not until a lumber company extended a road into the area in 1889 that an effort to mine the ore began. The ores were relatively low grade and the mines were closed from 1919 to 1941. During World War II the mines were reopened, but they were finally closed in 1978. At their peak in 1960 they employed 840 people.

As you drive on NY 3 east of the hamlet of Star Lake, you can see millions of tons of mine waste rock from the highway on the north side of Little River, which is between NY 3 and the Benson Mines. It is possible to enter the Benson Mines area via the old railroad tracks that enter the mine area from the west. As you follow the old rail tracks you can see the former mine area and highwalls, which are now a huge lake. A large waste rock pile with minerals that include pyrite, chalcopyrite, magnetite, garnet, phlogopite, and other minerals is located just south of the rail tracks. An abandoned railcar is just north of the waste rocks and is a convenient landmark. The waste rock pile is one of many in the area, and it is easy to spend a significant amount of time at this pile looking for interesting minerals. Many of the rocks are laced with pyrite and chalcopyrite, and this makes for some interesting patterns on the rocks. There are also reportedly several large abandoned buildings to the east, but I did not go into this area.

This rock has some deep red garnets and pyrite, and was found on the ground near the large waste rock pile.

References: Palmer, 1970; Robinson and Chamberlain, 2007; Hagni, 1968; Hagni et al., 1969; Hall, 2005

60. Fine Roadcut Titanite, Pyroxene, and Purple Fluorite

Light green pyroxene and crystals of purple fluorite can be found at this outcrop, as well as resinous titanite and flakes of biotite.

(See map on page 156.)

County: St. Lawrence County

Site type: Roadcut outcrops

Land status: Private, not posted

Material: Titanite, pyroxene, purple fluorite

Host rock: Metasedimentary gneiss

Difficulty: Moderate

Family-friendly: No, limited area, specialty minerals

Tools needed: Hammer, chisel

Special concerns: Roadcuts require some climbing

Special attractions: None

GPS parking: N44° 14' 39" / W75° 07' 59"

Topographic quadrangle: Fine, NY

Parking is adequate along this roadcut and this road sees relatively little traffic.

Finding the site: From I-81, take exit 44 to Watertown, and go through the town until you reach NY 3E. Continue on NY 3E for approximately 45 miles, and turn left (north) onto NY 58N. Take the very first right (east), and proceed down this road about 0.2 mile. The outcrops are on the right (south) side of this road, just west of the bridge that crosses the Oswegatchie River.

Rockhounding

Mineral collectors will find this site interesting even though the collecting areas are relatively small. The minerals are generally confined to the coarser-grained areas of the metasedimentary gneisses, and you can see where previous rockhounds have exposed coarse-grained zones in the outcrops. You will also have to climb onto the outcrops to reach the mineralized zones. The minerals at this site include titanite, which is also known as sphene, light green pyroxene, and grains of purple fluorite. Some of the rocks also have some distinct microcline crystals, and these are generally light tan. With some work you may be able to find some nice pieces, especially if you are able to find an exposure that has not been worked by previous mineral collectors.

References: Robinson and Chamberlain, 2007

61. Hailesboro Banded Marble Road Cut

This piece of white marble was found on the ground near the roadcuts.

(See map on page 156.)

County: St. Lawrence
Site type: Roadcut
Land status: Uncertain, may be in road right-of-way, not posted
Material: Bedded marble
Host rock: Marble
Difficulty: Easy
Family-friendly: No, collecting very limited
Tools needed: Hammer
Special concerns: Traffic and parking
Special attractions: None
GPS parking: N44° 18' 41" / W75° 27' 15"
Topographic quadrangle: Gouverneur, NY

The banded marble outcrops are a prominent feature along Highway 58 between Gouverneur and Hailesboro.

Finding the site: From I-81, take exit 48 to I-781/Fort Drum Connector, continue about 4.3 miles, and take exit 4 to US 11. Proceed on US 11 for about 34 miles to the town of Gouverneur, and turn right (south) on NY 58. The outcrops are exposed in about 1 mile, and the site referenced here is approximately 1.9 miles south of the intersection of US 11 and NY 58. Be sure to park in an area that is well away from traffic.

Rockhounding

The banded marble outcrops on NY 58 are very impressive and have undoubtedly been seen by many rockhounds as they travel through St. Lawrence County. They are bright white and have folded beds. It is possible to look at these closer to see the marble and bedded zones, and small chunks of white marble can sometimes be found at the base of the roadcuts. The roadcuts are mostly solid rock and can be damaged by hammering, so it is best to observe and photograph the cuts and leave any collecting to loose material that is already on the ground.

References: Rogers et al., 1990

62. Balmat Sylvia Lake Talc

Piles of waste rock from the mine line the southeast side of the road near Sylvia Lake.

(See map on page 156.)
County: St. Lawrence
Site type: Waste rock piles
Land status: Public fishing access
Material: Talc and wollastonite
Host rock: Dolomitic metasediments
Difficulty: Easy
Family-friendly: Yes
Tools needed: Hammer, small shovel
Special concerns: Very limited collecting, pieces very small
Special attractions: Sylvia Lake fishing
GPS parking: N44° 15' 01" / W75° 24' 20"
Topographic quadrangle: Gouverneur, NY
Finding the site: From I-81, go through Watertown and take NY 3E to Harrisville. Harrisville is approximately 35 miles from Watertown. In Harrisville, turn left (north) on NY 812. Proceed 8.6 miles, and turn left onto Pumphouse Road. There is a sign near the entrance indicating that this is a public fishing access area, but you

Small pieces of talc and tremolite can be found in the piles.

will have to drive past some of the mine buildings to get to the lake. Follow this road to where it ends at the lake. Small piles of white rock are along the southeast side of the road next to Sylvia Lake.

Rockhounding

This site is the principal talc mine in the Balmat area. Ideally one would be able to get access to the mine or find larger piles of waste rock, but this site is easily accessible and offers the opportunity to get some pieces of talc. The site is a fishing access point for Sylvia Lake, and piles of waste rock are on the southeast side of the road. The piles are probably some of the mine spoils that have been placed along the roadside. They have apparently been picked over by previous collectors, so it may be necessary to dig into the piles to get better pieces. Look for the small bladed white pieces, which are generally flat and shiny. If you can scratch them with your fingernail you have found some talc. There are also small pieces of tremolite in the piles, as well as some sulfides. If you do make any holes, be sure to cover them immediately so that the area looks as good as it did when you arrived.

References: Robinson and Chamberlain, 2007

63. Talcville Tremolite and Talc

Mine Road continues into the woods, and white rocks with tremolite and minor talc can easily be found on the road.

(See map on page 156.)

County: St. Lawrence

Site type: Loose rocks on road

Land status: Uncertain, not posted, may be public road

Material: Tremolite and talc

Host rock: Precambrian marble and gneiss

Difficulty: Easy

Family-friendly: Yes

Tools needed: Hammer, chisel

Special concerns: Land status uncertain, insects

Special attractions: None

GPS parking: N44° 18' 51" / W75° 17' 44"

GPS road section with minerals: N44° 18' 52" / W75° 17' 58"

Topographic quadrangle: Edwards, NY

Finding the site: From I-81, take exit 48 to I-781/Fort Drum Connector, continue about 4.3 miles, and take exit 4 to US 11. Proceed on US 11 for about 34 miles

to the town of Gouverneur, From Gouverneur, take NY 58S, and go about 10.3 miles to CR 97/Talcville Road. Turn left (north), and follow Talcville Road 1.7 miles through Talcville. Look for a very slight left turn (you cannot turn here if heading west) up Mine Road. It is a very rough road, but it improves slightly as you go up the hill. Go about 0.1 mile, and park in the parking area on the right (east) side of Mine Road. From here you can walk up the road to the tremolite/talc rocks in the road. The main mine area, which I did get to visit, is reportedly just east of the parking area, but I am uncertain of the status for access.

This piece with radiating tremolite crystals was found along the road.

Rockhounding

Much of the area around Talcville is private and posted land. I was originally about to give up on finding an accessible area, but I took a drive up Mine Road to the area of the International Talc Mine, which is a former talc mine northeast of Talcville. This mine operated from the late nineteenth to the mid-twentieth century. Mine Road is not well maintained but I had no problem driving up this road, and I parked in a small parking area on the east side of the road. Technically the road appeared to still be a public road, and I did not see any signs posting the surrounding area against trespassing. There were loose white rocks in the area, indicating that other rockhounds had also been here. I walked down the road, hoping to find a mine, but did not find it. I instead found that some parts of Mine Road had been covered with many white rocks that contained radiating tremolite crystals. The tremolitic rocks in general did not have any talc. As I walked eastward back to my car on Mine Road, I noticed that some parts of the road, especially when the rocks became a little grayer, had rocks with talc and anthophyllite. I also found some concrete foundations but no additional rocks. I later found out, using Google Maps, that the main mine area was just east of my parking area. If I had just headed east I would have likely found the main mining area. I am not sure of the status of the mine, but as mentioned I did not see any "no trespassing" signs in the immediate area, so it is certainly worth a look if you visit this site.

References: Robinson and Chamberlain, 2007

64. Harrisville Mine Blue Calcite and Wollastonite

Blue calcite is abundant and found as rounded pieces on the roadside near the gate.

(See map on page 156.)
County: Lewis
Site type: Waste rock near mine entrance
Land status: Private, not posted
Material: Blue calcite and wollastonite
Host rock: Metasedimentary dolomites and gneisses
Difficulty: Easy
Family-friendly: Yes, but only when mine is not active
Tools needed: Hammer, chisel
Special concerns: Active mine site, truck traffic near gate
Special attractions: None
GPS parking: N44° 07' 17" / W75° 22' 38"
Topographic quadrangle: Natural Bridge, NY
Finding the site: From I-81, take exit 44 to Watertown, go through the town until you reach NY 3E. Continue on NY 3E for approximately 29.1 miles, and turn left

Blue calcite and white wollastonite can be found in the waste rock outside the mine entrance gate.

(north) onto CR 7, which is Hermitage Road. The entrance to the mine is on the left. Proceed past the entrance, make a U-turn, and park on the right (west) side of Hermitage Road near the gate. The waste rocks are most abundant near the gate and are also present near some large boulders placed on the side of the road approximately 300 feet north of the gate.

Rockhounding

Active and former mines, while you may not be able to get permission for access, often have an abundance of interesting rocks and minerals stockpiled near the mine entrances. As long as you are not causing a traffic problem or disturbing mine personnel, you can gener-

ally look at these rocks, and they often are well worth your time. At this site you can find an abundance of light blue calcite and white wollastonite outside the mine gate and along the west side of Hermitage Road. While the calcite is generally easy to break with a standard rock hammer, the wollastonite is extremely hard and durable and is very difficult to break with a hammer.

References: Robinson and Chamberlain, 2007

This is a typical piece of wollastonite from the entrance.

65. Oxbow Road Calcite

This is a typical large rock with calcite that can be found at this roadcut.

(See map on page 156.)
County: St. Lawrence
Site type: Roadcut
Land status: Private, not posted
Material: Calcite
Host rock: Precambrian marble and Potsdam Sandstone
Difficulty: Easy
Family-friendly: Yes
Tools needed: Hammer, chisel
Special concerns: Road traffic, land status uncertain
Special attractions: None
GPS parking: N44° 19' 05" / W75° 37' 54"
Topographic quadrangle: Muskellunge Lake, NY
Finding the site: From I-81, take exit 49 for NY 411, and follow 411E for 3 miles. Continue straight onto NY 26S for 1.7 miles into the town of Theresa, and turn left onto Commercial Street. Continue onto Mill Street for 0.6 mile, turn left onto

This small rockpile at the base of the roadcut is loaded with calcite.

Oxbow Road, go 0.4 mile, and continue on CR 22 for 9.2 miles. Turn left (north) onto CR 25, go 0.7 mile, and turn left onto Oxbow Road (this is a completely different Oxbow Road than the one mentioned earlier). This road is also shown as CR-3/Rossie-Oxbow Road on Google Maps. Continue 1.3 miles, and look for a long, broken-up roadcut on the east side of the road. Pull well over to the side of the road and park. The calcite is found throughout much of this roadcut.

Rockhounding

This roadcut was first exposed when the road was widened in the 1960s. Some voids in the Precambrian marble host rock had excellent calcite specimens, and collectors have been working this site since it was first discovered. The local township apparently took a dim view of collecting and covered parts of the outcrop and excavations with black tar, which ruined many specimens. Today the tar can still be seen, but the calcite is still very abundant. The outcrop extends for more than 100 feet along the side of the road, and you can see lots of areas where rockhounds have broken apart rocks and left many interesting pieces for future collectors. This is an excellent place for a brief stop if you want to quickly see some calcite. Much of the calcite is white to tan, but some clear crystals can be found with a little effort.

References: Robinson and Chamberlain, 2007; Walter and Chamberlain, 2009

66. Yellow Lake Roadcut Calcite

Plates with good calcite crystals can still be found at this roadcut.

(See map on page 156.)
County: St. Lawrence
Site type: Roadcut
Land status: Private, adjacent to road
Material: Calcite
Host rock: Precambrian marble
Difficulty: Easy
Family-friendly: No, space is somewhat limited, land status questionable
Tools needed: Hammer, chisel
Special concerns: Traffic on road, land status
Special attractions: None
GPS parking: N44° 21' 05" / W75° 35' 54"
GPS roadcut: N44° 21' 07" / W75° 35' 49"
Topographic quadrangle: Natural Dam, NY
Finding the site: From I-81, take exit 49 for NY 411, and follow 411E for 3 miles. Continue straight onto NY 26S for 1.7 miles into the town of Theresa, and turn

The area with the calcite is slightly recessed relative to the rest of the roadcut, and parking is available just southwest of the mineralized zones.

left onto Commercial Street. Continue onto Mill Street for 0.6 mile, turn left onto Oxbow Road, go 0.4 mile, and continue on CR 22 for 9.2 miles. Turn left (north) onto CR 25, go 0.7 mile, and stay to the right (northeast) to continue on CR 10 (Rossie-Macomb Road). The roadcut with the calcite is approximately 3.8 miles farther on this road, and is on the left (northwest) side of the road, just opposite the only house on this road.

Rockhounding

This site is a road cut that appears to have resulted from the widening of the road in the early 1960s. Significant mineralized voids in the exposed marble contained crystals of calcite and dolomite. Goethite, pyrite, marcasite, siderite, and quartz were also reported at the roadcut. The highway department had to fill in some of the voids, and by far the best collecting opportunities at the site have long been gone. However, as of 2013 there were still pieces of rock with calcite and dolomite crystals, and some of the rocks near excavated areas have orange and white calcite crystals exposed in the outcrops. I was able to find some nice pieces with calcite crystals near the side of the roadcut. However, it is important to note that this is directly across the street from a house, and you must be careful to not bother the occupants with hammering or other noise.

References: Chamberlain and Walter, 2006

67. Whetstone Gulf Fossils

This is a typical weathered fossiliferous rock from the creek bed.

County: Lewis
Site type: Loose rocks in streambed
Land status: State park, no collecting allowed
Material: Brachiopods and crinoids in siltstone, trilobites and graptolites in shale
Host rock: Brown siltstone (formation unknown) and Utica Shale
Difficulty: Easy
Family-friendly: Yes
Tools needed: None
Special concerns: No collecting, some hiking
Special attractions: Whetstone Gulf (Gorge)
GPS western parking area: N43° 42' 03" / W75° 28' 33"
GPS creek area with fossils in brown siltstone rocks: N43° 41' 59" / W75° 28' 43"
GPS Utica Shale outcrops: N43° 42' 07" / W75° 28' 03"

Sites 67–68

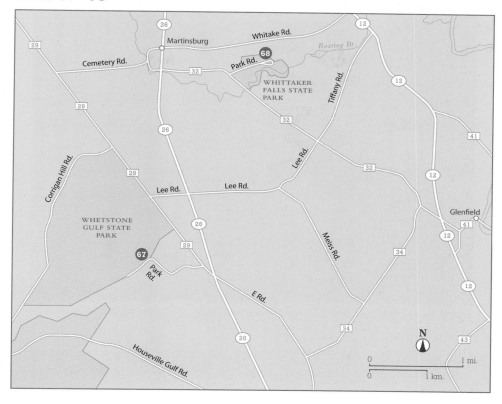

Topographic quadrangle: Glenfield, NY

Finding the site: From I-81, take exit 42 for NY 177. Continue approximately 25.7 miles east to NY 12S and stay to the right. Continue 2.8 miles to South State Street, turn right (west), go 0.5 mile, and stay right (south) on NY 26S. Go about 5.7 miles, turn sharply right (northwest) onto CR 29, go 0.1 mile, and take the next left (west) into Whetstone Gulf State Park. Pay the vehicle entrance fee and you can proceed to the GPS coordinates for the Utica Shale, which are just south of the road, and the GPS coordinates for the western parking area, which is next to a trail that goes upstream and to an area with abundant fossils in loose brown siltstones.

Rockhounding

Whetstone Gulf is a huge gorge within Whetstone Gulf State Park. Since it is a New York state park, fossil collecting is not allowed, but the site is still known for trilobites and graptolites in the Utica shale, and brachiopods and

Many of the rocks along Whetstone Creek are loaded with brachiopods and crinoids.

crinoids can be seen in loose rocks along Whetstone Creek west of parking area at the end of the road into the park. This site is an excellent place to bring kids and others who want to see fossils, as they are very abundant in the loose brown siltstones west of the parking area. It is also relatively safe as you are at the bottom of the gorge. The Utica Shale is easily accessed as well, but I found that the fossils were relatively scarce in this area. I found a partially pyritized graptolite and a fragment of a trilobite in the Utica Shale, but that was it. While fossil collecting is not allowed, the park is very scenic and is still worth a visit to see the fossils if you are in the area.

References: None

68. Whittaker Falls Brachiopods

The bumps on these limestone slabs in Roaring Brook are the tops of brachiopods

(See map on page 183.)
County: Lewis
Site type: Loose rocks in streambed
Land status: Town park and private land
Material: Brachiopods
Host rock: Ordovician King Falls Limestone of the Trenton Group
Difficulty: Easy, but difficult access to streambed
Family-friendly: No, hiking may be too intense
Tools needed: Hammer
Special concerns: Steep cliffs, hiking through woods, land status questions
Special attractions: Whetstone Gulf State Park
GPS parking: N43° 44' 07" / W75° 26' 47"
GPS bottom of gorge: N43° 44' 01" / W75° 26' 35"
Topographic quadrangle: Glenfield, NY
Finding the site: From I-81, take exit 42 for NY 177. Continue approximately 25.7 miles east to NY 12, and stay to the right (south). Continue 2.8 miles to South State

This is the base of Whittaker Falls as seen from the bottom of the gorge in Roaring Brook.

Street turn right (west), go 0.5 mile, and stay right (south) on NY 26S. Go about 3.3 miles, and turn left onto Glendale Road. Go about 0.8 mile, and turn left onto Park Road. You will see a sign for "Whitaker Park," but note that the spelling is missing the second "t." Park Road takes you into Whittaker Park. Proceed to the end of the road, staying to the right, and park at one of the parking spots in the woods. Walk downslope to the trail that roughly parallels Roaring Brook and heads east. Go past the fence (the area north of the trail past the fence is apparently posted land) and look for a faint trail that descends to Roaring Brook. There are multiple trails, all of which are questionable, so try to pick the best one. Be extremely careful, as this area is very steep and slippery.

Rockhounding

Whittaker Falls is within a town park that is owned by the Town of Martinsburg. This site has many large, flat plates of limestone that are often full of brachiopods. Even though they are flat, they are not shaly, and do not split well, so a chisel is not very useful at this site. The best fossils are found on weathered surfaces. Many of the best pieces are found loose in Roaring Brook, which is the stream that forms Whittaker Falls and the gorge. During my visit to the area in July 2013, it was a rainy day, and the water was quite high. I parked

Many loose flat rocks with abundant brachiopods can be found on Roaring Brook below Whittaker Falls.

in the parking area near the campgrounds and walked on the trail that went downstream and apparently past the falls. I passed a fence that had a sign indicating that the land behind the fence was posted, but the trail was not fenced off, and I was uncertain if this meant that the woods left (north) were private or if this is where the town land stopped. Since the path was very well worn, I continued on the trail east and looked for an area to descend to the stream. I finally found a very poorly defined path downslope, and it was quite steep and slippery, but I finally made it to the stream. Apparently I had descended to the area below the falls, as I could only see the bottom section of the falls. The bottom of the streambed had many interesting pieces of limestone with protruding brachiopods. I did not find any pieces that were in original outcrops. The area was quite rugged and I had to go into water up to my knees to get around the banks of the stream. I later found out that I had missed the actual trail to the falls. Reportedly there is another trail farther upstream that leads directly to the falls, and this may be a better trail to take, as it is likely on town land and you do not have to take this steep hike.

References: Kay, 1937; Fisher et al., 1970

69. Thacher Park *Zoophycos* and Brachiopods

The quarry floor is covered with the trace fossil *Zoophycos*.

County: Albany

Site type: Former quarry and escarpment

Land status: John B. Thacher State Park

Material: *Zoophycos* trace fossils and brachiopods

Host rock: Devonian Esopus shale, Oriskany Sandstone, Becraft Limestone

Difficulty: Easy

Family-friendly: Yes

Tools needed: None

Special concerns: No collecting, moderate hike to cliffs, large crevasses in rocks off trail, must stay away from edge of crevasses and cliffs

Special attractions: Additional hikes in Thacher Park

Sites 69–74

Brachiopods are common in loose rocks along the trail.

GPS parking: N42° 40' 36" / W74° 02' 51"
GPS cliff viewing area: N42° 41' 08" / W74° 02' 11"
Topographic quadrangle: Altamont, NY
Finding the site: From the Albany area, get on US 20W and take NY 146W toward Altamont. Go about 6 miles to Altamont, continue on Main Street for another 0.6 mile, and continue on NY 156 for 1.3 miles. Turn left (south) on Old Stage Road, proceed 1.2 miles, and turn left (east) onto Carrick Road. Continue on Carrick Road for about 0.3 mile and turn left (northeast) on a small road. Follow this road to the quarry, which is a very broad, flat area. From here you can park and walk to the trails to the cliffs.

Rockhounding

John Boyd Thacher State Park is a popular park that is only 12 miles west of Albany. The park is located along the Helderberg Escarpment, one of the richest fossil-bearing formations in the world. Although collecting is not allowed, it is still worth visiting the park to see *Zoophycos* trace fossils, brachiopods, and the view of the Helderberg Escarpment. This site is

The floor of the former quarry makes an excellent parking area.

in the northern section of the park, and the parking area is the floor of a former quarry.

The trace fossil *Zoophycos* covers the floor of the quarry. This is not the actual animal, but rather its trace that was left by brushing along the sediment. It appears as feathery plumes and is very easy to see. After parking at the quarry, you can hike approximately 1.5 miles to a viewing point from the cliffs of the Helderberg escarpment. The Helderberg escarpment defines the western edge of the Hudson Valley, and you can see the buildings of the Empire State Plaza in Albany to the east. On the trail you will encounter several loose rocks with fossils. Many of these have rounded brachiopods that protrude from the surface of the rocks, and they are easy to see on the surface. The top of the escarpment also has some very large crevasses formed from cracking and erosion of the upper bedrock surface, and some of these are very deep. Make sure that you stay on the trail to avoid stepping into one of these deep fractures, as you could easily break a leg, twist an ankle, or fall in and not be able to get out.

References: Isachsen, et al., 2000; Rogers et al., 1990

70. Schoharie Rickard Road Fossils

This is a typical piece of fossiliferous gray limestone that can be easily found at this site.

(See map on page 189.)

County: Schoharie

Site type: Roadcut

Land status: Uncertain, not posted

Material: Fossils, very abundant

Host rock: Lower Devonian Kalkberg and Becraft Limestones of the Helderberg Group

Difficulty: Easy

Family-friendly: Yes

Tools needed: Hammer, chisel

Special concerns: So many fossils that it is difficult to know where to focus

Special attractions: Howes Caverns

GPS parking: N42° 39' 47" / W74° 17' 55"

Topographic quadrangle: Schoharie, NY

The Becraft Formation forms the cliffs, while the Kalkberg Formation is exposed in the lower slopes.

Finding the site: From I-88, take exit 23 for NY 30A towards Schoharie. Turn left (south) on NY 30A, go 0.9 mile, and take a slight right to NY 30S and continue for 2.7 miles. This becomes Main Street in Schoharie. Turn left (south) onto CR 1b/Prospect Street, and go 0.7 mile. Prospect Street soon becomes Rickard Hill Road. The outcrops are on your left (north). Make a U-turn and park at a safe place on the roadside.

Rockhounding

This is a very large roadcut that has abundant fossils, and it is a very safe place for collecting. The Becraft Formation is the unit that forms the rock wall and talus at this cut. It is a coarse-grained massively bedded limestone. The Kalkberg Limestone is a thin to medium-bedded limestone with shale, and forms the broad flat surface exposed below the walls. Both units are fossiliferous. It is very easy to find fossils on the weathered surfaces of the limestones. The fossils are so numerous that is it difficult to know where to start. I first focused on finding some large flat slabs that were full of fossils, but I found that most of the rocks were too small or already broken, and it was difficult to find slabs. I later concentrated on finding pieces with large numbers of fossils that were exposed on weathered surfaces. I had more success with this, and found some very nice pieces. This area is reportedly the site of many field trips, so you are also likely to see signs of former visitors during your visit to this site.

References: Grabau, 1906

71. North Blenheim Schoharie Creek Fossils

Bivalves are common fossils at this location.

(See map on page 189.)

County: Schoharie

Site type: Roadcut/streambank

Land status: Uncertain, not posted

Material: Fossils, mainly bivalves

Host rock: Shale

Difficulty: Easy

Family-friendly: Yes

Tools needed: Hammer, chisel

Special concerns: Have to walk near road, some climbing on streambank

Special attractions: NYS Power Authority Pumped Storage Power Project

GPS parking (fishing access): N42° 29' 59" / W74° 25' 08"

Topographic quadrangle: Gilboa, NY

Finding the site: From I-88, take exit 23 to NY 30S through Schoharie. Continue on NY 30 for approximately 8.6 miles. The parking area is a small fishing access

The cliffs make it easy to find this site, but do not collect along the cliffs. Instead, look for fossils below the cliffs along the east bank of Schoharie Creek.

point on the right (west) side of the road. The shale outcrops are a sheer cliff on the left (east) side of NY 30 above Schoharie Creek just south of the boundary for the hamlet of North Blenheim. Park at the access and walk south to an area where you can climb down to the creek.

Rockhounding

This is a very easy site to find, as the shale cliffs cannot be missed as you are driving on NY 30. The shale has some minor fossiliferous zones, but it is far too dangerous to collect at the base of the cliffs. There is practically no space to be safe from cars approaching from the south if you are along the site of the cliff. Whenever you are faced with a locality like this, it is always best to look downhill for a safe place. At this locality you can climb down to Schoharie Creek, and the shale is exposed beneath the concrete alongside NY 30. Look for fossil-bearing zones in the shale and in loose rocks. I found some of the best pieces in loose rocks just north of the access point in a grassy area along the bank. Unfortunately this area is undoubtedly full of ticks and poison ivy, so you have to be careful. Collecting may also be difficult during periods of high water along Schoharie Creek. Parking is safe and adequate for a few vehicles at the fishing access point, but it should be noted that this is marked as fishing access only.

References: Zabriskie, 1999

72. Leesville Highway 20 Fossils

At this site the best fossils are found on weathered surfaces of the limestone.

(See map on page 189.)

County: Schoharie

Site type: Roadcut

Land status: Uncertain, not posted, may be in highway right-of-way

Material: Brachiopods, sponges, bryozoans, crinoids, trilobites also reported

Host rock: Kalkberg Limestone of the Lower Devonian Helderberg Group

Difficulty: Easy

Family-friendly: Yes

Tools needed: Hammer, chisel

Special concerns: Traffic on highway

Special attractions: None

GPS parking: N42° 47' 57" / W74° 39' 06"

Topographic quadrangle: Sprout Brook, NY

Finding the site: From I-90, take exit 29 towards NY 10. You will go through the town of Canajoharie, so follow the signs to stay on NY 10S. After you go through the town, continue approximately 9.5 miles on NY 10 south to the intersection with NY 20 in the small town of Sharon Springs. Turn right (west) onto NY 20, and proceed 1.7 miles to the roadcuts. The parking area recommended here is on the north side of NY 20, and parking at this site was adequate.

Rockhounding

This roadcut exposes the Kalkberg Limestone of the Lower Devonian Helderberg Group. This is a thin to medium-bedded, fine-to-medium light gray limestone with shaly beds. The rocks were deposited in well-agitated deep water at or near the normal wave base. Fossils are extremely abundant in the Kalkberg Limestone, and nearly all of the rocks at this roadcut have indications of fossils. The rocks are exposed on both sides of NY 20, but due to the traffic I stayed on the northern side. Some of the best fossils can be found by searching the weathered limestone surfaces rather than by breaking open the rocks. The rocks and fossils here are similar to those found at the Schoharie Rickard Road locality (Site 70).

References: Grabau, 2006

Parking is adequate near the roadcut and the collecting zones are well away from traffic.

73. Cherry Valley Highway 20 Corals

This location is easy to spot by the large fallen blocks along Highway 20.

(See map on page 189.)

County: Otsego

Site type: Roadcut with fallen blocks

Land status: Uncertain, not posted

Material: Corals

Host rock: Middle Devonian Edgecliff Member of the Onondaga Limestone

Difficulty: Easy

Family-friendly: Yes, but only small groups

Tools needed: Hammer, chisel

Special concerns: Traffic on NY 20

Special attractions: Glimmerglass State Park

GPS parking: N42° 49' 21" / W74° 43' 32"

Topographic quadrangle: Sprout Brook, NY

Finding the site: From I-90, take exit 29 towards NY 10. You will go through the town of Canajoharie, so follow the signs to stay on NY 10S. After you go through the town, continue approximately 3.3 miles on NY 10S to the intersection with NY 163W (Sprout Brook Road). Turn right (west) onto NY 163W, proceed 2 miles, and turn left (south) onto Cherry Valley Road. Continue another 0.3 mile and stay to the right on Cherry Valley Road as the road forks. Proceed 3 miles, and the road becomes NY 166S near the intersection with US 20. Continue 0.2 mile, and make a sharp right to merge onto US 20E. Continue 0.7 mile, and there will be an area to

This coral was found loose on the ground next to the fallen blocks.

pull off on the right (south) side of US 20. The site is at the large blocks that have fallen off the cliffs, and they are next to the highway.

Rockhounding

This site offers an interesting opportunity to collect corals in limestone. The lowest member of the Onondaga Limestone, known as the Edgecliff Member (a very appropriate name for this locality) is exposed above the underlying Carlisle Center Formation of the Lower Devonian Tristates Group. Several large blocks of the Edgecliff Member have fallen from the cliff and have excellent assemblages of rugose and tabulate corals. They are generally best exposed on weathered surfaces of the limestone, and there are many loose pieces with coral fossils along the base of the cliffs. The large sections that are exposed in the blocks are virtually impossible to remove with a hammer, and should be left for future visitors to experience.

The underlying Carlisle Center Formation consists of thin- to medium-bedded sandy siltstones, and does not contain any fossils with the exception of the trace fossil *Zoophycos*. This is believed to be the feeding trace of a worm, and consists of broad, sweeping "brush strokes" on the rock surface. I saw a few *Zoophycos* fossils at this site, so they should be relatively easy to find if you look for them in addition to the corals.

References: Lieb and Grasso, 1990

74. Fly Creek/Cooperstown Highway 28 Fossils

The fossiliferous rocks at this site generally have aggregates of brachiopods along bedding planes.

(See map on page 189.)
County: Otsego
Site type: Roadcut
Land status: Private, likely in highway right-of-way
Material: Brachiopods and bivalves
Host rock: Middle Devonian Panther Mountain Formation
Difficulty: Easy
Family-friendly: No, traffic is too heavy
Tools needed: Hammer, chisel
Special concerns: Land status, heavy traffic on NY 28
Special attractions: Cooperstown Baseball Hall of Fame
GPS parking: N42° 42' 35" / W74° 57' 15"
Topographic quadrangle: Cooperstown, NY

Finding the site: From I-88, take exit 17 for NY 28N, and proceed 17.3 miles to Cooperstown. From here, turn left (west) and continue on NY 28N/NY 80W for 1.5 miles. The outcrops will be on your left. Drive past this area, make a U-turn, and proceed back on the road to a broad parking area that will be on the right (south) side of the road. This road gets a lot of traffic, so be extremely careful when crossing the road to the outcrops.

Rockhounding

At first glance this site appears to be mainly barren shale and siltstone, but among the loose rocks you can often find large slabs of fossils that formed on bedding planes. The fossils in these slabs are generally small brachiopods, and they can number in the hundreds. Towards the eastern end of the roadcut, there is an outcrop largely covered by trees that has several large weathered slabs with fossils on their surface. Please note that much of this area is also posted ground, so be sure to stay out of the areas that are marked against trespassing. An orange safety vest is highly recommended for this area, and if at all possible you should try to visit this site when traffic is at a minimum.

References: Isachsen, et al., 2000; Van Diver, 1985

The outcrops are small and difficult to spot, but look for them on the north side of the road where the road has a slight bend to the southeast.

75. Brookfield Beaver Creek Road Fossils

These brachiopods were found by breaking apart loose rocks along the quarry highwall.

County: Madison
Site type: Former roadside quarry
Land status: Beaver Creek State Forest
Material: Brachiopods, bivalves, trilobites
Host rock: Middle Devonian Delphi Station Member of the Skaneateles Formation
Difficulty: Easy
Family-friendly: Yes
Tools needed: Hammer, chisel, screwdriver
Special concerns: State forest land, area overgrown during summer, insects
Special attractions: Beaver Creek State Park
GPS parking: N42° 50' 31" / W75° 18' 56"
Topographic quadrangle: Brookfield, NY
Finding the site: This site is well away from the major interstates and is best approached by starting in the small town of Brookfield. From the center of

Sites 75–78

The quarry is overgrown, and while the floor is flat, the drainage ditch next to the highway will likely keep all but the highest clearance vehicles from entering the site.

Brookfield, simply take Beaver Creek Road north for 2.1 miles, and look for a broad opening on the left (west) side of the road. This is the former quarry. Parking is best in a very small area on the east side of the road. You can also park in the floor of the former quarry, but the drainage ditch between the road and the quarry may prevent you from entering if you have a vehicle with low clearance, and this is not recommended.

Rockhounding

This former quarry has fossils that are similar to those found at other regional roadcuts in the shales and siltstones of the Delphi Station Member. I found that many of the rocks were barren, and it took some effort to find fossils at this site. I was there in midsummer, and the area was heavily overgrown, and the bugs were quite fierce. The best way to find the fossils, as at similar sites, is to simply look in the talus slopes along the highwalls and break open the rocks with fossils. I was able to find some brachiopods, but did not find any trilobites. With luck you may be able to find trilobites at this site, as they are reported from this locality.

References: Grasso, 1986

76. Hamilton Briggs Road Quarry Fossils

The circular pattern is a *Zoophycos* trace fossil, and these are relatively common in Devonian sediments in New York.

(See map on page 203.)
County: Madison
Site type: Small borrow pit next to road
Land status: Private, but not posted
Material: Brachiopods, crinoids, *Zoophycos* trace fossils
Host rock: Middle Devonian Ludlowville Formation Shale of the Hamilton Group
Difficulty: Easy
Family-friendly: Yes
Tools needed: Hammer, chisel, flat-bladed screwdriver
Special concerns: Land status uncertain
Special attractions: None
GPS parking: N42° 47' 27" / W75° 36' 04"
Topographic quadrangle: Hamilton, NY
Finding the site: This site is far away from all the interstate highways so the directions are simply given from the town of Hamilton. From Hamilton, head west

The pit is on the north side of Briggs Road and is easy to see from the road, which is visible in the left side of this photo.

on Lebanon Street. This soon turns into Randallsville Road. Turn left (south) on River Road, and go 0.5 mile and turn right (west) onto Briggs Road. Continue on this road for 1.6 miles, and the quarry, which is really a roadside borrow pit, will be on your right just before the crest of the hill.

Rockhounding

It is relatively easy to find and access this borrow pit, which has good examples of brachiopods, crinoids, and the trace fossil *Zoophycos*. The best way to find the fossils is to walk throughout the pit and look for larger pieces with indications of fossils on the surface, then split them open along bedding planes. Large bivalves are reported to be in the upper parts of the quarry in the coarser sediments, but I did not see any significant differences in the upper or lower zones of the quarry. There are also fossiliferous rocks in the bedrock surfaces exposed on the sides of Briggs Road adjacent to the quarry, but you must make certain that you avoid traffic and do not damage the road by removing any rocks.

Brachiopods are easy to find at this site.

References: Oliver and Klapper, 1981

77. Hubbardsville Cole Hill Road Fossils

This trilobite was found in rocks on the north side of the quarry next to the woods.

(See map on page 203.)

County: Madison

Site type: Roadside borrow pit

Land status: Private, not posted

Material: Brachiopods, crinoids, trilobites

Host rock: Middle Devonian Delphi Station Member, Hamilton Group

Difficulty: Easy

Family-friendly: Yes

Tools needed: Hammer, chisel

Special concerns: Land status uncertain

Special attractions: None

GPS parking: N42° 50' 56" / W75° 25' 43"

Topographic quadrangle: Hubbardsville, NY

The quarry is on the west side of Cole Hill Road and has lots of space for parking.

Finding the site: From US 20, head to the small town of Sangerfield. At Sangerfield, turn south onto NY 12, go 4.6 miles, and turn right (west) onto Swamp Road. Go 1.2 miles and turn left (south) onto Mason Road, which becomes Cole Hill Road. Proceed about 0.4 mile to the site, which will be to your right (west). Adequate parking is available.

Rockhounding

This is a well-exposed roadside quarry. Much of the shale and siltstone at this site is barren, and you have to look for the pieces with small vugs and bedding planes that may indicate the presence of fossils. I spent quite a bit of time breaking rocks apart. Shortly after I arrived I got lucky and found a trilobite in some of the rock piles on the northern side of the quarry. I also found quite a few brachiopods and crinoids, but despite considerable effort I was not able to find another trilobite.

References: Waite et al., 2004

78. Morrisville Swamp Road Fossils

Brachiopods are common at this site.

(See map on page 203.)

County: Madison

Site type: Roadcut

Land status: Uncertain, not posted

Material: Brachiopods, crinoids, and other Devonian fossils.

Host rock: Devonian Bridgewater and Solsville members of the Marcellus Shale

Difficulty: Easy

Family-friendly: Yes

Tools needed: Hammer, chisel, flat-bladed screwdriver

Special concerns: Some climbing on hillside

Special attractions: None

GPS parking: N42° 56' 04" / W75° 39' 47"

Topographic quadrangle: Morrisville, NY

The shale at the base of the outcrop is barren, while the siltstones above the shale have numerous fossils.

Finding the site: From I-81, take exit 15 for US 20E. Follow US 20E for 15.3 miles through Cazenovia. After you exit Cazenovia, continue another 10.7 miles on US 20E to Cedar Street in Morrisville. Turn left (north), continue about 0.5 mile, and the road then forks. Stay to the right (east), and the road becomes Swamp Road. Swamp Road is also known as CR 101. Continue about 2.2 miles to the site, which is a large outcrop on the right (east) side of the road.

Rockhounding

This is an aptly named road, as it is right next to Morrisville Swamp. Fortunately, the sides of the road are very wide at this outcrop, and there is more than adequate parking. At first glance it looks like a hard place to find fossils, as the base of the outcrop is mainly dark shale. This is the Bridgewater member, and it is relatively barren of fossils. The Solsville member is light brown-to-gray calcareous shale and siltstone and is above the Bridgewater, and the Solsville is the unit with fossils. The most abundant fossils at this site are brachiopods and crinoids, but bryozoan, gastropods, and trilobites are also reported. The best way to find the most fossils is to climb up the shaly hillside to the talus slope that has broken up rocks of the Solsville member. Pick up the fossils and split them open along bedding planes, and you should quickly find some nice brachiopods and crinoids.

References: Bailey, 1983; Rollins et al., 1971

79. Chittenango Falls Calcite and Celestite

This rock with small clear calcite crystals was found in the area where the ground was not posted.

County: Madison
Site type: Roadside cliffs
Land status: Chittenango Falls State Park, no trespassing
Material: Calcite and celestite
Host rock: Silurian light gray dolomitic limestone
Difficulty: Easy
Family-friendly: No, cannot pass posted signs
Tools needed: None
Special concerns: "No trespassing" signs, no collecting, highwalls
Special attractions: Chittenango Falls State Park
GPS parking: N42° 59' 11" / W75° 50' 45"
Topographic quadrangle: Cazenovia, NY
Finding the site: From I-81, take exit 15 for US 20, and take US 20E for 15.3 miles. After you reach the town of Cazenovia, turn left (north) onto Forman Street, go 0.2

Sites 79–84

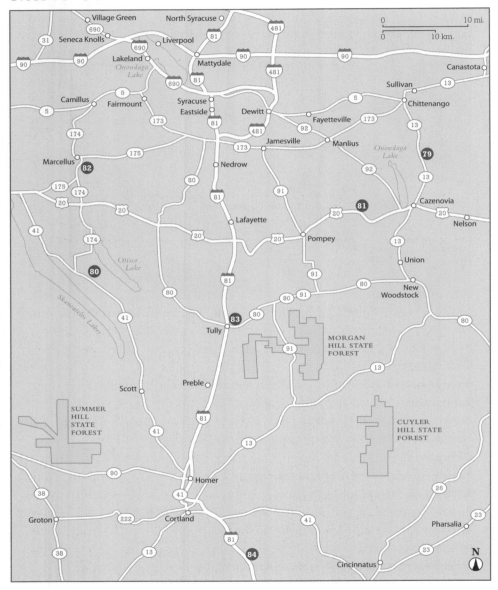

Village Green
North Syracuse
690
481
31
Seneca Knolls
690
Liverpool
81
Camillus
Lakeland
Mattydale
90
5
Fairmount
690
81
5
Syracuse
Eastside
Dewitt
Fayetteville
173
Jamesville
Manlius
Nedrow
92
81
91
Lafayette
Pompey
Union
80
81
80
91
New
Woodstock
80
80
Tully
83
80
91
MORGAN
HILL STATE
FOREST
Preble
Scott
SUMMER
HILL
STATE
FOREST
41
81
13
CUYLER
HILL STATE
FOREST
90
Homer
38
41
26
Groton
222
Cortland
41
23
38
13
81
23
Cincinnatus
Pharsalia

Onondaga Lake
90
90
90
481
5
Sullivan
Chittenango
Canastota
13
13
173
Onondaga Lake
79
92
13
175
80
Marcellus
82
173
173
175
174
20
20
81
20
Cazenovia
20
Nelson
41
174
13
Otisco Lake
80
Skaneateles Lake
80
91

0   10 mi.
0   10 km.

N

The cliffs, as well as the "no trespassing" signs, are easily visible from Highway 13.

mile, and turn right (east) onto Albany Street. Continue on Albany Street for 0.4 mile and turn left (north) onto Farnham Street, which turns into NY 13/Sweetland Street, also known as Gorge Road. Proceed 4.7 miles to the parking area, which will be on the left (west) side of NY 13. The cliff is on the right (east) side of NY 13 when heading north.

Rockhounding

This is a classic New York locality for calcite and celestite, but the State of New York has blocked access to even entering the site. The cliffs are right on the east side of NY 13, and there is a huge parking area on the west side of the highway, so it is easy to find and view from the roadside. Unfortunately, the east side of the road is heavily posted with signs that prohibit trespassing for any reason.

However, at the time of my visit to the site in May 2013, there was a small section south of the cliffs outside of the posted areas. This area had an abundance of tiny, clear calcite crystals and some vugs filled with dogtooth calcite. I did not see any celestite, but I am sure that I could have found some with more effort. As this is a state park, collecting is still not allowed, but at least I was able to walk over this area as I was outside of the no trespassing signs. There were several indicators that other rock collectors had recently been in the area, as many of the rocks were broken, and calcite crystals were strewn about the area. Even though collecting is not permitted, this is still an interesting locality to check out.

References: Robinson and Chamberlain, 2007; Thibault, 1935

Chittenango Falls Calcite and Celestite   **213**

80. Borodino Highway 41 Fossils

Some of the fossil-bearing zones are full of crinoids.

(See map on page 212.)

County: Onondaga

Site type: Roadcuts

Land status: Private, not posted

Material: Corals and crinoid fossils

Host rock: Devonian Tully Limestone

Difficulty: Moderate

Family-friendly: No, limited exposures, must walk along high-traffic highway.

Tools needed: Hammer, chisel

Special concerns: Traffic

Special attractions: Eastern Finger Lakes

GPS parking: N42° 51' 06" / W76° 19' 04"

GPS outcrops: N42° 51' 02" / W76° 18' 57"

Topographic quadrangle: Spafford, NY

Finding the site: From I-81, take exit 15 for US 20. Take US 20W for 12 miles, then turn left (south) on Rose Hill Road. This is shown on Google Maps as Rose Hill

The Borodino Mounds outcrop is on the east side of Highway 41 and is easy to identify as it is next to a sign indicating a highway curve.

Road, but is also labeled CR 211B, CR 27A, CR 21, and NY 174. Continue 5.4 miles on Rose Hill Road, and turn left (southeast) onto NY 41. Continue approximately 1.1 miles. The parking area will be on the left, and it is just north of the intersection of NY 41 with Willow Hill Road. From the parking area, walk several hundred feet south, and you will see limestone outcrops on both sides of the highway. Be extremely careful when walking along this highway.

Rockhounding

These exposures have been referred to as the Borodino Mounds complex, which is an unusual thickening in the upper part of the Devonian Tully Limestone. The complex was originally composed of lime muds deposited in a shallow shelf in a quiet environment. The deposition has been compared to the modern-day carbonate mud mounds on the shallow shelf in the Caribbean near northern Honduras.

Some sections of the limestone are massive and barren, while some are loaded with crinoids and corals. The best exposures are on weathered surfaces of the outcrop. While some loose material can be found near the outcrops, it is best to leave the most fossiliferous zones in the hard limestone intact so they can be studied by future visitors.

References: Heckel, 1973

81. Pompey Center Highway 20 Fossils

This brachiopod was found in loose rocks at the base of the roadcuts.

(See map on page 212.)
County: Onondaga
Site type: Roadcuts
Land status: Private, not posted
Material: Fossils
Host rock: Devonian Delphi Station Member of the Skaneateles Formation
Difficulty: Easy
Family-friendly: Yes
Tools needed: Hammer, chisel
Special concerns: Very limited parking
Special attractions: Chittenango Falls State Park
GPS parking: N42° 55' 24" / W75° 55' 48"
Topographic quadrangle: Oran, NY

The roadcut is easy to locate and it is possible to stay well away from traffic.

Finding the site: From I-81, take exit 15 for US 20E, which is also known as the Cherry Valley Turnpike. Proceed approximately 11.1 miles to the roadcuts, which are on the north and south sides of US 20 as it descends east from a large hill east of Pompey Center. The parking area is a very small space on the right (south) side of the road just west of the roadcuts, and you may very well pass this parking area as you are looking for the roadcuts. If you do, simply double back and park.

Rockhounding

The Delphi Station Member of the Skaneateles Formation is part of the Devonian Hamilton Group of sediments. It consists of soft, dark shales at the base and grades to sandy shales and hard calcareous sandstone near the top of the formation. Fossils are very common and include brachiopods, corals, bivalves, and bryozoans. The roadcuts extend for hundreds of feet on both sides of the highway, but I found the north side of the highway the most productive for finding fossils. Many good fossils are also found in loose material at the base of the roadcuts.

References: Brower and Nye, 1991

82. Marcellus Shale Type Section and Concretions

Large concretions are found at this roadcut, and while most are solid, some have calcite veining.

(See map on page 212.)

County: Onondaga
Site type: Roadcuts
Land status: Uncertain, not posted
Material: Black shale and large concretions
Host rock: Devonian Marcellus Shale
Difficulty: Easy
Family-friendly: Yes
Tools needed: Sledgehammer, hammer, chisel, flat-bladed screwdriver
Special concerns: Traffic on road
Special attractions: Eastern Finger Lakes region
GPS parking: N42° 58' 33" / W76° 19' 57"
GPS outcrop: N42° 58' 28" / W76° 20' 03"
Topographic quadrangle: Marcellus, NY

The Marcellus Shale at this locality is black and fissile, and crumbles very easily.

Finding the site: From I-81, take exit 15 towards US 11/US 20, and take US 20W (Cherry Valley Turnpike) 10.7 miles to Slate Hill Road. Turn north (right), and proceed 3.4 miles to the intersection with NY 174/175 (Lee-Mulroy Road). A parking area is available at the northwest corner of this intersection. The roadcuts of Marcellus Shale are located on the east side of NY 174/175 just south of this parking area. Do not attempt to park at the roadcuts, as the space between the roadcut and highway is not large enough to safely park a car.

Rockhounding

Welcome back from Mars if you have not heard of the Marcellus Shale. The Marcellus Shale has become one of the most famous shales in the world as a result of horizontal drilling, hydraulic fracturing, and the tremendous success that natural gas drillers have experienced in developing the Marcellus. In New York, the Marcellus Shale is considered a subgroup of the Devonian Hamilton Group, and the Marcellus subgroup is further subdivided into three formations, which are the Union Springs, Oatka Creek, and Mount Marion and several members.

This locality exposes the lower black shales of the Oatka Creek Formation of the Marcellus Shale. Due to its proximity to the town of Marcellus, this is sometimes considered the type locality for the Marcellus Shale. The type locality refers to a location where the exposures are best representative of the rocks of a particular stratigraphic unit. The shale at this location is dark black, flaggy, and very fissile, and easily flakes apart when picked up. It is hard to believe that billions of dollars have been invested in finding and developing this shale as a source of natural gas. The Utica Shale, which is also mentioned in this book, is also a target for natural gas drilling. At the time of this writing, New York still has a moratorium on developing the Marcellus and Utica Shales for natural gas, but the nearby states of Pennsylvania, Ohio, and West Virginia are moving ahead rapidly with development of this resource. It is ironic that the New York towns of Marcellus and Utica are the namesakes for these shales, and New York prohibits the development of shale gas.

In addition to being an outcrop where you can actually see the Marcellus Shale, these roadcuts contain very large concretions. Some of them are more than a few feet in diameter. They are extremely hard and are hard to break apart with a rock hammer. A sledgehammer might be the best way to break open the larger concretions. Most of them are solid, but some are septarian concretions that have septa of fine-grained orange carbonate, which I suspect is aragonite due to its bladed appearance. A flat-bladed screwdriver can be used to split the shale to find smaller concretions within the shale.

References: Hall, 1839; Ver Straeten et al., 2011

83. Tully I-81 and Highway 80 Fossils

This is a calcareous section of the shale that has brachiopods, crinoids, and some minor bryozoans.

(See map on page 212.)
County: Onandaga
Site type: Hillside
Land status: Uncertain, not posted
Material: Brachiopods
Host rock: Middle Devonian Windom Shale of the Moscow Formation
Difficulty: Easy
Family-friendly: Yes
Tools needed: Hammer, chisel
Special concerns: Land status uncertain
Special attractions: Labrador Hollow Unique Area (near Morgan Hill State Forest)
GPS parking: N42° 47' 56" / W76° 07' 15"
GPS hillside: N42° 47' 59.8" / W76° 07' 10"
Topographic quadrangle: Tully, NY

The hillside northeast of the motel is very broad and fossils are easy to find on the slopes.

Finding the site: This site is extremely easy to find. Take I-81 to exit 14, and turn east onto NY 80. Depending on which way you are approaching, you may turn onto NY 281 (if you are coming from the south) or US 11 (if you are approaching from the north) to get to NY 80. Immediately east of I-81 is a convenience store, motel, and drugstore. The outcrops are in the hillside behind the motel. This stop makes a great place to get gas, water, and drinks before fossil hunting, and if it is late you can also stay at the motel.

Rockhounding

This site exposes a broad area of the Windom Shale of the Moscow Formation. The fossils at this site lived in a muddy sea floor with relatively high sediment loads, and this is indicated by the abundance of bivalves and gastropods at the site. Some of the more limestone-rich zones in the shale also contain brachiopods and bryozoans. Corals are rare but have been reportedly found at this site. An additional fossiliferous exposure of the Windom Shale is reported to be present on the east side of US 11 just northwest of this hillside.

References: Rogers et al., 1990

84. Hoxie Gorge Fossils

Slabs with abundant brachiopods are easy to find in the stream.

(See map on page 212.)
County: Cortland
Site type: Streambanks
Land status: Uncertain, not posted
Material: Loose fossil plates with brachiopods in stream
Host rock: Upper Devonian Geneseo Formation shales
Difficulty: Easy
Family-friendly: Yes
Tools needed: Hammer, chisel, flat-bladed screwdriver
Special concerns: Land status uncertain, may get wet in stream
Special attractions: Hoxie Gorge Nature Preserve
GPS parking: N42° 32' 47" / W76° 05' 41"
Topographic quadrangle: McGraw, NY
Finding the site: From I-81, take exit 10 for US 11, and turn left (south). Proceed approximately 3.5 miles, and turn left (east) on Hoxie Gorge Road. You will immediately see the I-81 bridge that crosses Hoxie Gorge. Proceed 0.1 mile and

The fossils are found in the stream near the I-81 bridge.

you will see a small parking area where you can pull over. Park here and walk to the area of the stream under the I-81 bridge. Fossils are found in loose slabs along the bed and banks of the stream.

Rockhounding

This very easy site to find is in an interesting setting, as the massive I–81 bridge passes right over the gorge. The stream cuts through Upper Devonian shales of the Geneseo Formation of the Genesee Group. The outcrops themselves are relatively poor in fossils, but I found that there are abundant fossil "plates" of masses of brachiopods and related fossils. These occur as large and small slabs in the stream in Hoxie Gorge.

The site is also reported to contain specimens of a feather–like fossil, known as Plumalina plumeria. This is considered a difficult fossil to classify as it is not easy to assign it to a distinct animal group. It resembles a plant but is thought to be a colonial hydrozoan and related to corals and jelly fish, and was also considered to be a graptolite. I found it not only difficult to classify but hard to find, so I recommend that if you come to this site you focus instead on the excellent and abundant rocks in the stream that are full of fossils.

References: Rogers et al., 2000; Ruedeman and Raymond, 1916

85. Vestal Route 26 Fossils

Brachiopods can be found by breaking apart the shaly layers in the rocks at the base of the cliffs.

County: Broome
Site type: Roadcut
Land status: Uncertain, not posted
Material: Fossils, mainly brachiopods
Host rock: Upper Devonian West Falls Group shale and siltstone
Difficulty: Easy
Family-friendly: No
Tools needed: Hammer, chisel
Special concerns: Close to road, highwall, sparse fossils
Special attractions: Robert H. Treman and Oquaga Creek State Park
GPS parking: N42° 04' 29" / W76° 02' 31"
Topographic quadrangle: Endicott, NY
Finding the site: From I-81, take the exit for NY 17W. At the time of this writing the area was undergoing considerable construction, and it is uncertain what the exit number will be in the future. Continue on NY 17W, which is also known on Google Maps as the Southern Tier Expressway, for 7.7 miles, and take exit 67S to

Sites 85–87

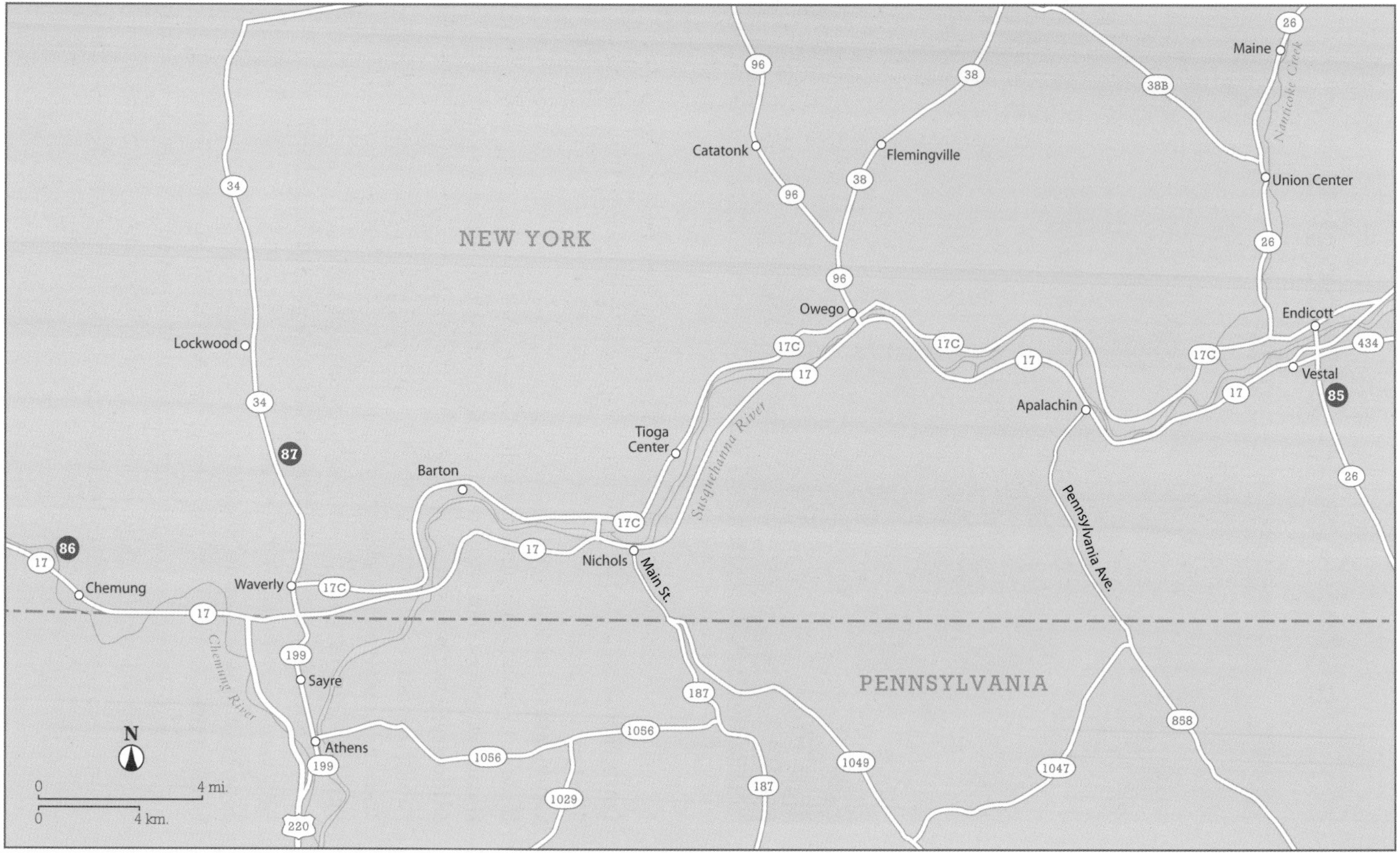

NEW YORK

PENNSYLVANIA

Nanticoke Creek

Susquehanna River

Chemung River

Maine

Union Center

Endicott

Vestal

85

26

434

26

26

17

17C

38B

38

Flemingville

38

96

Owego

Catatonk

96

96

Apalachin

Pennsylvania Ave.

858

1047

1049

17

17C

17C

17

Tioga Center

Main St.

Nichols

17C

187

187

1056

1029

1066

17

Barton

Sayre

Athens

199

199

220

17C

87

34

Lockwood

34

Waverly

17

Chemung

86

17

N

4 mi

4 km.

0

0

The cliffs are easy to spot along Highway 26.

NY 26S. In approximately 1 mile you will see a long, broad roadcut to your left (east). Make a U-turn and park on the east side of the road near the outcrop.

Rockhounding

This is an easily accessible outcrop in the Vestal Falls area, and parking is adequate for at least one car. The rocks are within the Upper Devonian West Falls Group, and the rocks at the outcrop are mainly shales and siltstones. Much of the rock does not contain fossils, but occasional zones of fossils can be found with some effort. Brachiopods are the most common fossils at this site.

References: Ehrets, 1980; Sorauf and Roberson, 1963

86. Chemung Narrows Former Highway 17 Fossils

This rock was split along a fossil-bearing zone and revealed several fossils.

(See map on page 226.)

County: Chemung

Site type: Roadcut

Land status: Uncertain, not posted

Material: Fossils, including brachiopods

Host rock: Upper Devonian West Falls Group

Difficulty: Easy

Family-friendly: Yes

Tools needed: Hammer, chisel

Special concerns: Highwalls, falling rocks, poison ivy, ticks

Special attractions: Watkins Glen State Park

GPS parking: N42° 01' 15" / W76° 38' 18"

Topographic quadrangle: Wellsburg, NY

Finding the site: From NY 17, take exit 59 at Chemung, and turn right onto Wyncoop Creek Road. Proceed about 0.2 mile and turn left (north) onto CR 60,

The Chemung Narrows is easy to find, and parking is on the east side of Highway 17C.

which is also known as Main Street. This used to be Highway 17, but has now been relegated to a back road that roughly parallels the new NY 17. This road is also sometimes referred to as Highway 17C. Proceed about 1.1 miles to the parking area on the right (east) side of the road. The cliffs extend for nearly 1,000 feet along the road from the parking area.

Rockhounding

This easy-to-find site also offers safe parking. The cliffs expose rocks of the "Chemung facies," which are shales, mudstones, siltstones, and fine sandstones of the Upper Devonian West Falls Group. These sediments were believed to have been deposited in a nearshore, subtidal shelf of the Catskill delta complex, which was a series of river deltas and marshy terrain between the former seas and former Acadian mountains. The fossils here are mainly molds and casts, and include brachiopods, pelecypods, corals, and crinoids. Many of the rocks are relatively barren, and you have to look for the fossil-bearing zones. Checking the loose rocks along the highwall will generally result in finding some fossils fairly quickly. The best way to find the fossils is to look for indications of molds and casts along the bedding planes. These are often indicated by a zone of small curved voids formed by the cross-sections of shells. Splitting these open with a chisel or hammer can often reveal some nice fossils.

References: Ehrets, 1981; McAlester, 1962; Rogers et al., 1990

87. Waverly Old Highway 34 Rugose Corals

This piece with weathered rugose corals was found in the ditch adjacent to the roadcut.

(See map on page 226.)
County: Tioga
Site type: Roadcut
Land status: Private, not posted
Material: Rugose corals
Host rock: Upper Devonian West Falls Group
Difficulty: Easy
Family-friendly: No, limited space on roadcut
Tools needed: Hammer, chisel
Special concerns: Limited parking, traffic
Special attractions: Watkins Glen State Park
GPS parking: N42° 03' 07" / W76° 32' 09"
GPS outcrop: N42° 03' 19" / W76° 32' 12"
Topographic quadrangle: Waverly, NY

The outcrops are right next to the road and you must be extremely careful at this site.

Finding the site: From Waverly, which is between Elmira and Binghamton along the New York-Pennsylvania border, take NY 34 north for 3.1 miles. Turn right onto Old Route 34. Parking is limited: There is space for just one car on the right as soon as you make this turn. Park here and walk to the coral-bearing outcrops, which are approximately 0.2 mile north of the parking area and are on the east side of the road.

Rockhounding

This is an easy-to-reach roadcut that has Upper Devonian rugose corals in siltstones and sandstones. Rugose corals, sometimes referred to as tetracorals, are extinct corals that were abundant through the Middle Ordovician to Late Permian. They are often shaped like a horn and have a wrinkled appearance. At this roadcut the corals are found in three narrow bands of cross-laminated sandstones and siltstones. The middle band is reported to be the most prominent and laterally extensive. I was unable to identify the specific bands, and focused on finding loose rocks on the ground. Some of the corals weathered in place and distinct cavities were formed as the corals were dissolved by groundwater. It is often possible to see the remnants of the horns in the weathered surfaces of the rocks. Make sure to stay outside any areas of posted ground, and stay well away from the traffic. Since this is Old Route 34, traffic is limited, but you still have to be very careful at this site.

References: Souraf, 1987

88. Portageville Highway 436 Road Aggregate Fossils

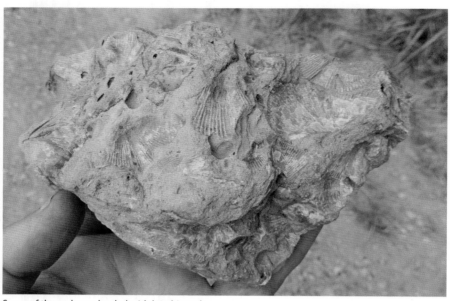

Some of the rocks are loaded with brachiopods.

County: Livingston
Site type: Loose coarse aggregate on hillside
Land status: Private, must stay next to road
Material: Fossils, mainly brachiopods
Host rock: Limestone
Difficulty: Easy
Family-friendly: Yes, but must stay away from traffic
Tools needed: Hammer
Special concerns: Private land, must stay out of posted areas
Special attractions: Letchworth State Park
GPS parking: N42° 34' 20" / W78° 02' 26"
Topographic quadrangle: Portageville, NY
Finding the site: From I-390, take exit 5 towards NY 36/Dansville, turn right (south), go about 0.8 mile, and turn right (west) onto NY 436W. Continue 19.2

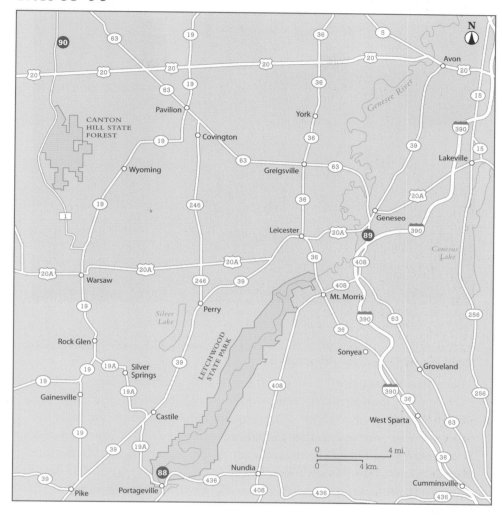

miles, and park at a parking area just south of the intersection of Totsline Road and NY 436. The parking area is just north of the Genesee River and is on the east side of the NY 436. The fossiliferous rocks are on the west side of NY 436, and several additional zones with fossil-bearing rocks can be seen farther north and east along NY 436.

The fossiliferous limestone is found among the rocks on the roadside.

Rockhounding

This is an unusual site in that it is not a naturally occurring fossil site. It basically consists of crushed and sized sandstone and limestone that have been placed to stabilize the hillside. I am not sure what formation the rocks are from, or their source, but they are almost certainly from a nearby quarry. Purists may protest inclusion of such a site in this guidebook, but the bottom line is that it has lots of fossils and offers the opportunity to find an abundance of brachiopods in limestones. If you need a site that offers the opportunity to immediately find some fairly large brachiopods, this is a good place to look. Simply walk along the roadside, being extremely careful of the traffic, and look for fossil-bearing limestones. Breaking them apart sometimes reveals some nice fossils, and I found a very large, nearly intact brachiopod by cracking apart a limestone with lots of fossils on its surface. However, bear in mind that the property away from the road is private, and be careful to stay out of posted ground.

References: None

89. Fall Brook Falls Brachiopods and Corals

This coral fossil was found by breaking open a loose rock of gray limestone in the stream valley.

(See map on page 233.)

County: Livingston

Site type: Outcrops and loose rocks along streambanks and cliffs

Land status: Private, not posted

Material: Brachiopods and corals

Host rock: Middle Devonian Moscow Formation and Upper Devonian Genesee Group

Difficulty: Easy

Family-friendly: Only for those with older kids with the ability to climb

Tools needed: Hammer, chisel

Special concerns: Dangerous drop over waterfall, steep cliffs, must climb down very steep trail to valley

Special attractions: Letchworth State Park

GPS parking: N42° 46' 30" / W77° 49' 39"

Topographic quadrangle: Geneseo, NY

Finding the site: From I-390, take exit 7 for NY 408 toward Geneseo/NY 63. Turn right onto NY 408, and stay to the left (north) as NY 408 turns into NY 63. Continue 1.1 miles north, and park at the parking area on the left (west) side of the road. There may be other cars parked here, especially on weekends. Take the trail at the parking area and stay to the right, and descend into the gorge below the falls. This is a very steep climb and unfortunately there is no other way to easily reach the valley. If you go to the left to the falls, be extremely careful, as there is no fall protection at the falls.

Fall Brook Falls is approximately 70 feet high and, though adjacent to Highway 63, can be seen only by hiking to the base of the falls.

Rockhounding

This site is a must visit if you are in western New York. There is a parking area on the road adjacent to the trails that lead to the stream gorge, and you can easily descend the trails to the falls. I say "descend," as it is a very quick and steep trip, and I highly recommend gloves to grab onto roots and trees and good hiking boots to get good purchase on the hillside if you visit this site. The best rocks for brachiopods and corals are the fossil-bearing gray limestones in the streambed. Break open these pieces and look for brachiopods and corals. A good hammer is important for this site. The best fossils are found by cracking open the limestones, as opposed to fossils on the weathered surface of the limestone. The Leicester pyrite bed, which is a pyritic zone between the Windom Shale of the Moscow Formation and the Geneseo Shale of the Genesee Group, is also exposed on the north side of the creek in a highwall just north of the falls. This pyrite bed is reported to contain fossils, but I did not find any significant fossils when I climbed up the shaly cliff to the pyritic zone. However, please also be aware that this site is on private land, and while it appears to be frequently visited, access to the site can change at any time.

References: Huddle and Repetski, 1981

90. East Bethany Francis Road Railroad Cut Fossils

It is easy to find horn corals, crinoids, and brachiopods on the hillside of the railroad cut.

(See map on page 233.)
County: Genesee
Site type: Shale bank along inactive railroad cut
Land status: Uncertain, not posted
Material: Small corals and brachiopods
Host rock: Middle Devonian shale of the Ludlowville Formation
Difficulty: Easy
Family-friendly: Yes
Tools needed: Small plastic bag for collecting fossils, flat-bladed screwdriver, garden trowel also useful; no hammer needed
Special concerns: Land status uncertain
Special attractions: None
GPS parking: N42° 55' 38" / W78° 09' 51"
Topographic quadrangle: Batavia South, NY

Finding the site: From I-90, take exit 48 towards Batavia. Turn left (south) onto Oak Street, go 1.1 miles, and turn left (southeast) onto West Main Street in Batavia. Go 0.3 mile, and the road turns into NY 63S. Continue southeast on NY 63S for 2.4 miles. Turn right (south) onto Shepard Road, go 0.6 mile, and stay right to continue on Putnam Road. Continue 0.7 mile, and take the first left (south) to Francis Road. Continue 2.2 miles south, and the parking area will be to your right. The fossil site is on the east of Francis Road on the north side of the hillside in a former railroad cut.

Rockhounding

This site is in a former railroad cut for the Delaware, Lackawanna & Western Railroad. The railroad connected Buffalo, New York, to Hoboken, New Jersey, and was incorporated in 1853. The railroad was profitable in the first two decades of the twentieth century, but reduced traffic in coal, competition from trucking, and high taxes hurt as the years went on. The railroad merged with the rival Erie Railroad in 1960 and was finally absorbed by Conrail in 1976. The tracks are long gone, and the railroad was one of many rail lines that gradually disappeared through industry consolidation and a shrinking market.

The Middle Devonian shale of the Ludlowville Formation, Hamilton Group is exposed in the cut. Fossils are found on top of the weathered slopes of the cut. During my visit to the cut in August 2013, I was able to quickly find several small fragments of rugose corals, brachiopods, and crinoids on the surface. I focused on finding the small corals, and although I checked some of the larger loose rocks in the cut, I did not find any significant fossils in them. The best and most numerous fossils are picked out with a sharp eye and your fingertips. You do not need a hammer, but a small plastic bag for the fossil pieces is highly recommended. This is a very good site for kids, as they should be able to find fossils very quickly. Unweathered shale from the top of the north bank also reportedly has trilobite fragments, but I did not find any at this site.

References: Drury, 1994; Eldredge, 1972; Rogers et al., 1990

91. Alden Spring Creek Trilobites and Concretions

This trilobite was found near the eastern end of the shale bank in loose shale in Spring Creek.

County: Erie

Site type: Outcrops along streambank

Land status: Private, not posted

Material: Trilobites, concretions, pyrite nodules also reported

Host rock: Middle Devonian Ludlowville shale

Difficulty: Easy

Family-friendly: Yes

Tools needed: Hammer, chisel, flat-bladed screwdriver, small shovel

Special concerns: Land status uncertain, muddy conditions

Special attractions: Niagara Falls

GPS parking: N42° 54' 06" / W78° 29' 10"

GPS shale outcrop: N42° 54' 12" / W78° 29' 02"

Topographic quadrangle: Corfu, NY

Sites 91–92

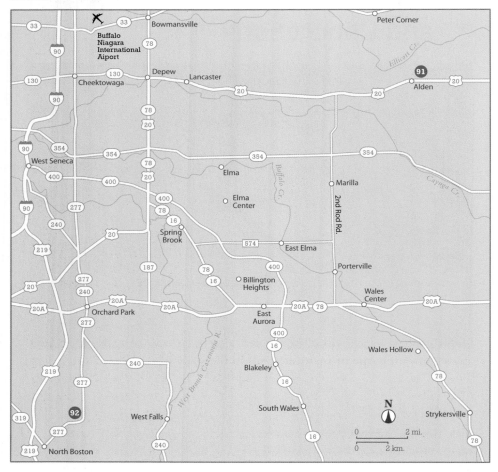

Finding the site: Take US 20 into the town of Alden. Turn north onto Westcott Avenue, and then make the first right (east) onto Irving Street. Proceed 0.2 mile to the end of Irving Street and park here, where a well-worn trail enters the woods. Follow the trail to Spring Creek; the shale bank outcrops are on the north side of the bank at the end of the trail.

Rockhounding

This site is fairly well known and is often referred to as the Alden pyrite beds. My main interest in this site was to find some pyritized fossils and nodules.

The shale bank on Spring Creek is at the end of the trail from Irving Street, and has lots of diggings from previous rockhounds.

Unfortunately, I have visited the Alden area twice and was unable to find any significant pyrite or marcasite beds in the shale banks I found on Spring Creek. During my first visit to the site, I hiked along Spring Creek from Crittenden Road, and did not encounter any significant shale beds or pyrite. During my last visit to the site I found an excellent trail to reach a prominent shale bank in Spring Creek, where several previous rockhounds had left many holes and obvious indications of digging. One of the excavations was filled with several large, (6 inches or more) solid, smooth concretions, and a couple of these were broken apart showing radiating patterns of calcite along fractures. I looked very hard in the shale outcrops and loose rocks in the stream, and I found some trilobites, but no pyrite. The pyrite beds might be farther downstream or upstream, but I did not have the opportunity to check them out. Although I did not encounter any pyrite at this shale bank, it is still worth visiting for the trilobites and concretions with calcite. The pyrite beds may be exposed in a nearby area of Spring Creek, and these directions will at least get you to the parking area and allow you to access the trails along the creek.

References: Domagala and Selznick, 1979; Chamberlain, 2007

92. Chestnut Ridge Park Eternal Flame

The Eternal Flame is natural gas that burns under a waterfall.

(See map on page 240.)

County: Erie

Site type: Waterfall with natural gas flame

Land status: Erie County Park

Material: Sandstones and Siltstones

Host rock: Devonian West Falls Group sediments

Difficulty: Easy

Family-friendly: Yes

Tools needed: None

Special concerns: Strenuous hike that may be difficult for some people, no collecting

Special attractions: Lake Erie, Niagara Falls

GPS parking: N42° 42' 07" / W78° 44' 51"

GPS eternal flame: N42° 42' 06" / W78° 45' 06"

Topographic quadrangle: Hamburg, NY

Finding the site: From the Buffalo area, head south on US 219, and take the Armor Duells Road exit. Turn right (east) on New Armor Duells Road, go about 0.7 mile, and turn right (south) onto NY 275S/Chestnut Ridge Road. Continue 3.2 miles, and look for a large parking area on the right. This will likely have many cars. From here, follow the trail to the eternal flame.

Rockhounding

This is a natural gas seep that burns with a distinct flame under a waterfall. This site is not for rockhounding, but it is included in this guide, as it is one of the most unique geologic features in New York. Given the worldwide concerns about energy, natural gas, and the environment, this site is all the more relevant. However, for many of those who could care less about the news and world events, it is still pretty neat to see a natural flame under a waterfall. Apparently many other people think so, as the parking lot must have had more than fifty cars during my 2013 visit on Sunday of Memorial Day weekend.

The trail appears to be well marked, and it was quite busy, so I have no good excuse for taking the wrong trail to the site, but I did. I made it to the flame but I took the long way. The trail can be very tricky, so pay close attention to the markers, which are small flames on selected trees next to the trail. When I got to the end of the trail there was almost always a line to take pictures next to the flame. The hike to the flame, while very easy for some people, is quite difficult for many. The trail, especially in the area of the creek, often had fallen trees that were difficult to climb over, or under, depending on the circumstances. I met one couple who were not in the best of shape, and they were very concerned about the climb out. The number of people that visit this site is all the more surprising when you consider the effort they take to get here. It is well worth a visit, especially if you can combine it with other rock-collecting or tourist trips in the Buffalo area.

References: Rogers et al., 1990

93. Chautauqua Creek-Lyons Road Fossils

Casts of brachiopods can easily be found in the loose rocks in the creek.

County: Chautauqua
Site type: Creek bed
Land status: Private, but appears to be frequently visited by locals
Material: Fossils, mainly brachiopods
Host rock: Gray siltstones and shales, Ellicott Member of the Chadakoin Formation
Difficulty: Easy
Family-friendly: No, mainly because of questions about land status
Tools needed: Hammer, chisel
Special concerns: Land status possibly an issue, posted grounds in woods
Special attractions: Chautauqua Lake
GPS parking: N42° 13' 35" / W79° 35' 39"
Topographic quadrangle: Sherman, NY
Finding the site: It is important to remember that Lyons Road ends at Chautauqua Creek in both directions. The bridge that crossed the creek was

Site 93

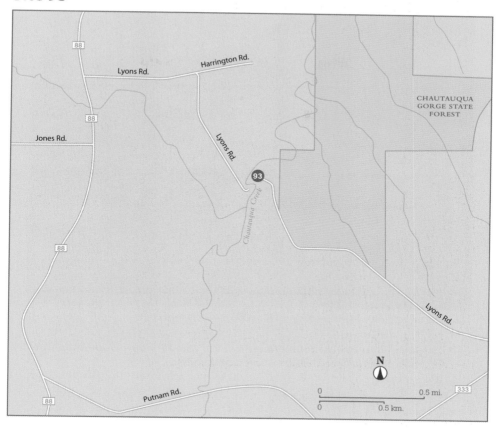

washed out, and I found it easiest to reach the site via the south side of the creek near Chautauqua Gorge State Forest. From I-86, take exit 6 for NY 76 toward Sherman. Turn north onto NY 76N/Osbourne Street, go 0.2 mile, and turn right (east) onto NY 430E/East Main Street, and continue 4.7 miles. Turn left (north) onto CR 333, go 0.2 mile, and turn right (north) onto Lyons Road. Follow Lyons Road 1.7 miles to the parking area at the end of road. Park here and walk to the creek. The fossils are easily found in the creek bed.

Rockhounding

It is very easy to find fossils at this site. The bottom of the creek bed has many large, flat rocks with protruding brachiopods, and many of the fossils are found as casts. The easiest way to find fossils is to simply look in the creek

Gray siltstones and shale are well exposed on the banks of Chautauqua Creek.

bed for large pieces with lots of brachiopods. I was not able to access any of the outcrops due to the water next to them, but I found more than enough interesting pieces in the creek bed. I tried to split some of the rocks, but they did not split apart very easily. However, they would easily crack open with a hammer. Many of the fossiliferous rocks occur as large slabs, and these are typically covered with casts of brachiopods, many of which are greater than an inch in diameter. Although the area is posted, three teenagers came down to the creek when I was at the site, and at least one other car came to the parking area. The path to the site was extremely well worn as well, which indicated that the area is often accessed. If you do come to this site, be aware that it is private land, albeit with parking and a trail, and that any site work or collecting is at your own risk.

References: Baird and Lash, 1990; Tesmer, 1963

ONTARIO LOWLANDS

94. Ontario Furnaceville Hematite

Pieces of hematite-rich rock can be found along the shoreline and in the woods.

County: Wayne
Site type: Former open-pit mine
Land status: Casey Park
Material: Hematitic fossiliferous oolitic sandstone
Host rock: Lower Silurian sediments of the Clinton Group
Difficulty: Easy
Family-friendly: Yes
Tools needed: None
Special concerns: Steep shorelines next to lake, no collecting
Special attractions: Fishing at Casey Park Lake
GPS parking: N43° 14' 11" /W77° 17' 18"
Topographic quadrangle: Ontario, NY

Sites 94–95

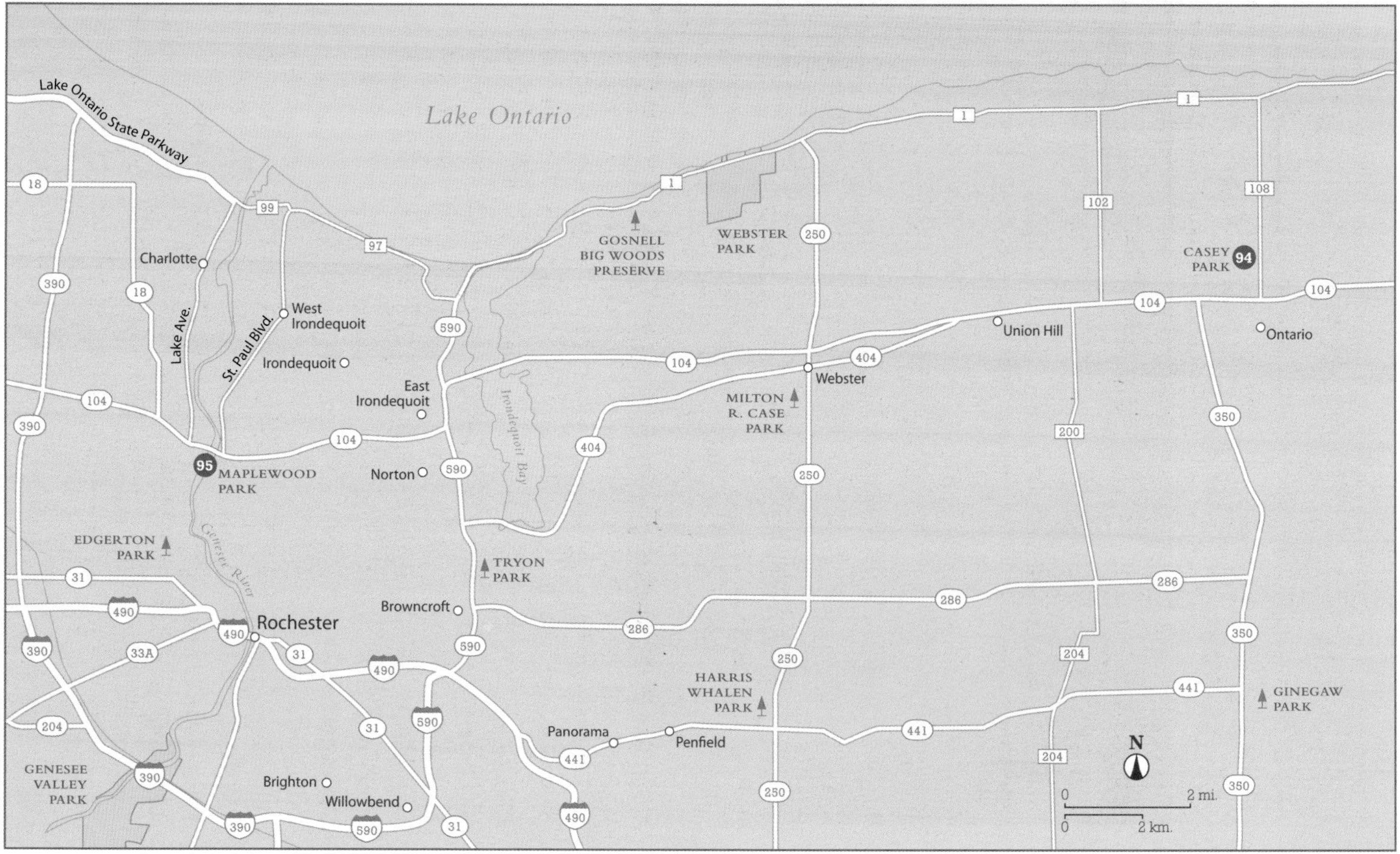

Lake Ontario State Parkway

Lake Ontario

GOSNELL
BIG WOODS
PRESERVE

WEBSTER
PARK

Charlotte

18

390

18

390

West
Irondequoit

Irondequoit

St. Paul Blvd.

Lake Ave.

East
Irondequoit

Norton

590

104

Genesee River

MAPLEWOOD
PARK

95

EDGERTON
PARK

Rochester

490

33A

31

GENESEE
VALLEY
PARK

204

390

590

Browncroft

490

31

Brighton

Willowbend

590

390

31

TRYON
PARK

Irondequoit Bay

590

286

Panorama

441

490

HARRIS
WHALEN
PARK

Penfield

250

441

286

Webster

404

250

250

204

MILTON
R. CASE
PARK

250

200

286

441

350

Union Hill

102

104

CASEY
PARK

94

Ontario

104

108

350

350

204

GINEGAW
PARK

350

N

0   2 mi.
0   2 km.

The former strip mine is now a large lake.

Finding the site: From I-90, take exit 43 toward NY 21N. Head north on NY 21 for 6.2 miles, and turn left (west) on NY 31. Go 1.2 miles, and turn right (north) onto CR 208/Walworth Road. Continue north for 11.4 miles, and turn left (west) onto Ridge Road. Go 0.2 mile, turn right (north) onto Knickerbocker Road, and continue for 1 mile, then turn left onto Casey Park Road. Enter Casey Park and park in one of the parking areas. You can hike to the lake from here. The hematitic ore can be found along the southern bank next to the Casey Harris Trail and at the western end of the lake. The street address for the park is 6551 Knickerbocker Rd., Ontario NY 14519. The park is open from 9 a.m. to dusk.

Rockhounding

This site was one of the main iron mines in the Ontario area in the late nineteenth century. The mine was developed to extract the red Furnaceville oolitic hematite ore that occurred in the Lower Silurian Clinton Group. The ores formed from the introduction of iron by surface waters after deposition of the sediments, which had an abundance of calcareous material from tiny marine fossils. These fossils acted as nuclei for oolitic coatings of hematite with chamosite. The iron eventually replaced the carbonates through diagenetic replacement and formed the beds of hematitic ore.

The former iron-mine workings are now a lake that is approximately a mile long and 200 feet wide. The mine was operated by the Furnaceville Iron Company from approximately 1870 to about 1900 and produced pig iron. The ores were generally about 43 percent iron and 0.5 percent phosphorous, which was a relatively high phosphorous content. This high phosphorous content was not good, as it would tend to make the iron brittle. The hematite ores occurred in a bed that was only about 22 inches thick, and about 22 feet of shale and overburden had to be removed to get to the hematite. About twenty tons of iron ore were produced daily, and it served the local Rochester, New York, market for manufacturing iron stoves and architectural iron products. Iron brackets, cornices, ornamental turrets, railings, fences, balconies and hitching posts were popular during the Victorian Era, and the local iron producers had a ready market. However, the very large iron ore deposits of the Mesabi Range in Minnesota were soon opened, and it became impossible for the Furnaceville deposits to compete. The deposits experienced a brief second life around 1900 as a pigment for red paint, which led to lots of red barns, but eventually this market ended and the mines closed.

Pieces of the hematite ore can be found along the shore of the lake. Unfortunately it is against the park rules to remove park property, but there are no restrictions on access to the areas with the hematite. I found numerous pieces of the hematitic sediments along the southern shore. The soils along the banks are often stained a slight red, and it is easy to find the former ores in the small drainages that lead into the lake. If you look closely at the rocks you can often see that some are red, and when you pick them up you will notice that they are extremely dense. They often have a red interior that is full of red microfossils and oolites. I did not see any of the hematitic ores in outcrop. I am certain that they are well below the bottom of the lake and covered with sediments, so do not waste your time looking for outcrops at this site.

References: Alling, 1947; Newland and Hartnagel, 1908; Schilling, 2002

95. Genesee River Gorge Hematite

The Furnaceville hematite is a red, fossiliferous oolitic sandstone that is very dense and easy to recognize.

(See map on page 248.)

County: Monroe

Site type: Outcrops in river gorge

Land status: City parkland

Material: Hematitic fossiliferous oolitic sandstone

Host rock: Silurian Clinton Group sediments

Difficulty: Moderate

Family-friendly: Yes

Tools needed: Hammer, chisel

Special concerns: Some hiking, steep drops, trip hazards

Special attractions: Genesee River Lower Falls

GPS parking: N43° 11' 14" / W77° 37' 23"

GPS hematite outcrop: N43° 11' 24" / W77° 37' 15"

Topographic quadrangle: Rochester East, NY

This hematitic layer is visible on the east side of the trail just downslope of Seth Green Drive.

Finding the site: This locality is in urban Rochester so there are a number of ways to approach the site. The best way is to get on Norton Street and head west to Seth Green Drive. At Seth Green Drive you will see the parking area to your left (south). Park here, and walk along Seth Green Drive until you see a wooden sign marking the Carthage Trail. Follow the trail down into the gorge. The hematitic outcrop will be to your right in the first several hundred feet along the trail, and you should use the GPS coordinates to find it, as it is only red in freshly broken areas.

Rockhounding

The hematitic fossiliferous oolitic sandstone that is exposed in the Genesee River Gorge is often referred to as the Furnaceville hematite. It is exposed in other sections of the gorge as well, but this is an area that is relatively accessible. The sandstone is distinct from the surrounding rock in that it is composed of many tiny fossils, including shells; has an oolitic texture; and is generally a dark brownish red ranging to red. Freshly broken surfaces are often a deep red. The outcrop referenced by the GPS coordinates is relatively small,

The Lower Falls of the Genesee River must be seen if you visit this site.

but there are other large outcrops of hematitic sandstone nearby in the gorge. The area also has a large tunnel that resembles a former mine, but I am not sure if this was constructed as a mine or built to assist with drainage in the area. If you look on the ground in the area, you can often find loose pieces of the hematitic sandstone. The Furnaceville hematite was mined and smelted to produce pig iron during the mid-1800s, but the discovery of vast iron ores in the Mesabi Range in Minnesota soon made it impossible for the Rochester area ores to compete as iron mines. However, near the turn of the twentieth century, the hematite was mined again to produce a red pigment for the paint industry. It was reportedly popular with farmers of the area, and this may have lead to the preponderance of red barns in the region. These mines eventually closed as other pigments were developed in the early twentieth century. The Furnaceville hematite mines are long gone, but the hematite is still very easy to find.

References: Gillette, 1947; Schilling, 2002

96. Penn Dixie Site Trilobites

This trilobite was found loose on the surface while splitting larger pieces of shale.

County: Erie
Site type: Former cement quarry
Land status: Private, fee-collecting site
Material: Trilobites, horn corals, brachiopods
Host rock: Devonian Windom Shale
Difficulty: Easy
Family-friendly: Yes
Tools needed: Sledgehammer, hammer, chisel, digging bar, flat-bladed screwdriver
Special concerns: Lack of shade, sunscreen and hat recommended
Special attractions: Niagara Falls
GPS parking (gate): N42°46' 33" / W78° 49' 50"

Sites 96–98

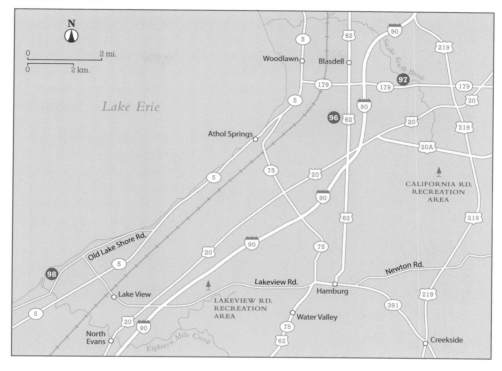

GPS main collecting area: N42° 46′ 43″ / W78° 49′ 55″
Topographic quadrangle: Buffalo SE, NY
Finding the site: From I-90, take exit 56 for NY 179/Mile Strip Road toward Blasdell. Go 0.5 mile and turn right (west) onto NY 179/Mile Strip Expressway, and go 0.2 mile. Turn left (south) onto NY 62S/South Park Avenue, and go 1.2 miles. At the traffic circle, take the first exit to the right (west) onto Big Tree Road, and go 0.3 mile. Turn right (north) onto Bristol Road, go 0.3 mile, and turn left (west) onto North Street. The gate will be approximately 0.1 mile farther on your right (north).

Rockhounding

The Penn Dixie site is one of the best places to collect trilobites. It is officially known as the Penn Dixie Paleontological and Outdoor Education Center, and is owned and operated by the Hamburg Natural History Society, a non-profit educational corporation. The site is a former quarry for calcareous

The Penn Dixie site is wide open and does not have any signficant highwalls.

shale that was operated by the Penn Dixie Cement Company. Quarrying ceased in the 1960s, and the shale that was removed exposed key fossil-bearing zones of Devonian trilobites, corals, brachiopods, and associated fossils. The site is open to the public during most daylight hours, and hours are posted on the society's website.

I had the opportunity to visit this site in May 2013 during a weekend visit to the Buffalo area. Any fossil collector or rockhound that passes through Buffalo should make it a point to visit this site if his or her schedule permits, as it is one of the few collecting places that you can access and have a good chance of finding large trilobites. At the time of my visit, a relatively new area of shale had been opened, and the experienced collectors were extracting and splitting large blocks of dark gray shale. Many of the pieces they split had large nests of trilobites, and I had never seen so many trilobites in a single rock outside of a museum setting. The operation reminded me of some of the mining that I have seen at Herkimer diamond sites, which involved splitting and breaking large blocks of dolomite to get to the pockets of Herkimer diamonds. However, the shale is much, much softer than the dolomite, and it is much easier to break out large slabs to find the trilobites. In addition to trilo-bites, you can find some excellent horn corals and brachiopods, but trilobites are generally the main focus of collectors at the Penn Dixie site.

This site is visited by collectors from around the world and should con-tinue to produce trilobites for many years to come. Since this is a unique collecting site, make sure you have the proper tools for collecting, as sum-marized in the tools needed section. Hard hats are not needed, but there is no shade at the collecting areas, so I also highly recommend sunscreen and a hat. Strong gloves are also recommended, as the shale tends to dry out your hands. While many fossils can be found by splitting the shale, you should also keep your eyes open for large trilobites and corals that are found loose on the ground. Even without breaking rocks you are likely to find many interesting fossils on the surface.

References: Brett, 1974; Buehler and Tesmer, 1963

97. South Branch Smokes Creek Fossils

This piece with some small trilobite fragments and a horn coral was found next to the shale bank.

(See map on page 255.)
County: Erie
Site type: Streambank
Land status: Uncertain, not posted
Material: Small trilobites and brachiopods
Host rock: Devonian Windom Shale
Difficulty: Easy
Family-friendly: Yes
Tools needed: Hammer, flat-bladed screwdriver, plastic bag for collecting
Special concerns: Part of hike in creek, wet feet
Special attractions: Niagara Falls
GPS parking: N42° 47' 29" / W78° 47' 39"
GPS shale bank with fossils: N42° 47' 26" / W78° 47' 39"
Topographic quadrangle: Buffalo SE, NY

The fossils are found in a shale bank located approximately 300 feet south (upstream) of the parking area.

Finding the site: From I-90W, head south to exit 52A, and keep right to follow US 219S, and continue for 3.4 miles. Take the NY179/Mile Strip Road W exit, and continue 0.7 mile to Abbott Road. Turn right (north) on Abbott Road, and park at the lower (west) parking area of the Newton Abbott Fire Company. This is a large parking lot that is well away from the fire trucks. You can walk to Smokes Creek and the fossil-bearing shales from here.

Rockhounding

The fossils are found as loose fragments in a large shale bank that is approximately 300 feet south (upstream) of the parking area. The shale bank is located on the west side of the stream at a broad curve where the stream bends to the east. The best way to find the fossils is to look for loose fragments at the base of the bank and within the bank itself. The shale is very loose, so you can easily pull many pieces of shale from the bank with your hands or a hammer, but you must be careful to make sure that you do not cause any damage to the bank. This site is easy to find and reach with a short upstream hike, but you will likely get wet, as you have to hike in the creek. You are likely to find fossils very quickly, so this is a good place to take kids and adults that may have a limited collecting horizon before they get bored.

References: Brett, 1974; Buehler and Tesmer, 1963

98. Eighteen Mile Creek Fossils

The base of the cliffs has many blocks of limestone as well as assorted lakeshore debris.

(See map on page 255.)
County: Erie
Site type: Lakeside cliffs
Land status: Uncertain, not posted
Material: Fossils, including trilobites, corals, and brachiopods
Host rock: Wanakah Shale and Tichenour Limestone of Middle Devonian Hamilton Group
Difficulty: Moderate
Family-friendly: Yes
Tools needed: Hammer, chisel, flat-bladed screwdriver
Special concerns: Some hiking to reach cliffs, quickly changing weather
Special attractions: Lake Erie
GPS parking: N42° 42' 41" / W78° 57' 59"
GPS lakeside cliffs: N42° 43' 04" / W78° 58' 09"
Topographic quadrangle: Eden, NY

These trilobites were found in loose shale in the cliffs at the mouth of Eighteen Mile Creek.

Finding the site: To get to the site from Buffalo, take I-90W south towards Erie, and take exit 57, which is NY 75, towards the west, and turn south onto US 20. Continue approximately 4.4 miles and turn a slight right onto Lakeview Road, and follow this west for approximately 2.25 miles until you reach the end of Lakeview Road with its intersection at Old Lake Shore Drive. Turn left (south) on Old Lake Shore Drive, and in about 1.2 miles you will cross Eighteen Mile Creek. The parking area is on the left (east) side of the road on the southwest side of the creek.

Approaching from Pennsylvania, take exit 58 from I-90E, which will take you to the intersection of US 20 and NY 5. Take NY 5W for approximately 12 miles, and turn left at South Creek Road, which is just before Eighteen Mile Creek. Take South Creek Road for approximately 0.25 mile, and then turn right (north) on Old Lake Shore Drive. The parking area will be on the right (south) side of Old Lake Shore Drive approximately 500 feet past this intersection.

From the parking area, walk north and back over the bridge, and look for an obscure trail north of the bridge and on the west side of the road. This trail leads along the northern side of the Eighteen Mile Creek. It crosses a small drainage and shortly afterwards will lead you to the mouth of the creek and the cliffs.

Rockhounding

This is great location that has safe parking and tremendous views of Lake Erie and nearby cliffs. The cliffs along the shoreline of Lake Erie at the mouth of Eighteen Mile creek consist of sediments of the Middle Devonian Hamilton Group. The Hamilton Group rocks along the base of the shoreline are mainly from the Wanakah Shale and Tichenor Limestone. The Wanakah Shale consists of medium gray, soft, fossiliferous shale and shaly mudstone with calcareous bands and zones of concretions. The Tichenor Limestone is much thinner, and is a resistant, ledge-forming unit above the Wanakah Shale.

Trilobites and smaller brachiopods can be found in the shale, while corals, crinoids, and larger brachiopods are abundant in the limestone. Most of the trilobites that I have found during my trips to this site were in the shale just east of the cliffs along the north side of Eighteen Mile Creek, and many of them were very small and in fragments. I found many excellent brachiopods, and also found many pyritized fossils in loose rocks that fell from the cliffs. The best way to find the fossils is to get large pieces of shale and split them with a small chisel or screwdriver, and you will almost certainly find fossils very quickly.

References: Beard, 2011

REFERENCES CITED

Adams, Arthur G. *The Hudson River Guidebook*. New York: Fordham University Press, 1996.

Alling, Harold L. *The Adirondack Graphite Deposits*. New York State Museum Bulletin 199. Albany, NY, 1917.

————. "Diagenesis of the Clinton Hematite Ores of New York." *Geological Society of America Bulletin* 58, no. 11 (1947): 991–1018.

Bailey, J. B. "Middle Devonian Bivalvia from the Solsville Member (Marcellus Formation), Central New York State." *Bulletin of the American Museum of National History* 174 (1983): 193–326.

Baird, G. C. and G. G. Lash. "Devonian Strata and Paleoenvironments: Chautauqua County Region, New York State." In *Field Trip Guide for the 62nd Annual Meeting of the New York State Geological Association,* A1–A46. Fredonia, NY: SUNY, 1990.

Bartolome, P. "Genesis of the Gore Mountain Garnet Deposit, New York." *Economic Geology* 55 (1960): 255-77.

Beard, Robert. "Eighteen Mile Creek Fossils: Cliffside Collecting on Lake Erie in New York State." *Rock & Gem Magazine* 41, no. 3 (March 2011).

————. "Staten Island Minerals: Take the Ferry to an Urban Field Trip." *Rock & Gem Magazine* 38, no. 6 (June 2008).

Beck, Lewis C. *The Mineralogy of New York*. Albany: New York: W. & A. White & J. Visscher, 1842. Facsimile reprint. Special Publication no. 2. Rochester, NY: Rochester Mineralogic Symposium, 1987.

————. *Second Annual Report of the New York State Cabinet of Natural History, Comprising Notices and Additions Which Have Been Made Since 1842*. Albany, New York, 1849.

————. *Third Annual Report of the New York State Cabinet of Natural History, Comprising Notices and Additions Which Have Been Made Since 1842*. Albany, New York, 1850.

Bennington, J. Bret. *Regional Geology of Southeastern New York State for Teachers and Travelers*. Hempstead, NY: Hofstra University, 2003.

Betts, John. "Anthony's Nose, New York: A New Look at an Old Location." *Matrix: A Journal of the History of Minerals* 5, no. 4 (1997): 131–43.

————. "Manhattan Mineral Collecting." *Mineral News* 14, no. 1 (1998):1-8.

Brett, C.E. "Stratigraphy and Paleoecology of the Windom Shale Member (Moscow Formation) in Erie County, New York." In *Field Trip Guide for the 46th Annual Meeting of the New York Geological Association,* G1–G15. Fredonia, New York: SUNY, 1974.

Brower, J. C. and O. B. Nye Jr. "Quantitative Analysis of Paleocommunities in the Lower Part of the Hamilton Group near Cazenovia, New York." In *Dynamic Stratigraphy and Depositional Environments of the Hamilton Group (Middle Devonian) in New York State, Part II,* eds. E. Landing and C. E. Brett, 37–74. New York State Museum Bulletin 469. Albany, NY, 1991.

Buddington, A. F. "Report on the Pyrite and Pyrrhotite Veins in Jefferson and St. Lawrence Counties, New York." *New York State Defense Council Bulletin,* no. 1 (1917): 23–25.

Buddington, A. F. and B. F. Leonard. *Regional Geology of the St. Lawrence County Magnetite District, Northwest Adirondacks, New York.* United States Geological Survey Professional Paper Series 376. Washington, DC: US Government Printing Office, 1962.

Budnik, Roy T., Jeffery R. Walker and Kirsten Menking. "The Geology and Topography of Dutchess County." Chapter 3 in *Natural Resource Inventory of Dutchess County, NY.* Report of Dutchess County, 2010.

Buehler, E J. and I. H. Tesmer. "Geology of Erie County New York." *Buffalo Society of Natural Science Bulletin* 21 (1963): 61–63.

Chamberlain, S. C. and M. Walter. "Road-Cut Mineral Occurrences of St. Lawrence County, New York, Part 2: Yellow Lake Road Cut." *Rocks & Minerals* 81 (September–October 2006).

Chamberlain, S. C., M. Walter, and R. P. Richards. "Phlogopite Triplets from the Selleck Road Occurrence, West Pierrepont, St. Lawrence County." In *Contributed Papers in Specimen Mineralogy: 38th Rochester Mineralogical Symposium Abstracts, Part 2,* 2011.

Chiarenzelli, J., M. Lupulescu, E. Thern, and B. Cousens. "Tectonic Implications of the Discovery of a Shawinigan Ophiolite (Pyrites Complex) in the Adirondack Lowlands." *Geosphere* 7 (2011): 333–56.

Clarke, John M. *Magnetic Iron Deposits of Southeastern New York.* New York State Museum Bulletin 249–50. Albany, NY, 1921.

Conklin, Lawrence H. "Kingsbridge, An Early Quarrying District on Manhattan Island." *Mineralogical Record* 28, no. 6 (November–December 1997): 457–73.

Cosminsky, P. R. "A Trip to Mt. Adam and Pine Island, Orange County, New York." *Rocks & Minerals* 22, no. 3 (1947): 207–9.

Cushing, H. P., and R. Ruedemann. *Geology of Saratoga Springs and Vicinity.* New York State Museum Bulletin 169. Albany, NY, 1914.

Darling, R. S., F. P. Florence, G. W. Lester, and P. R. Whitney. "Petrogenesis of Prismatine-Bearing, Metapelitic Gneisses along the Moose River, West-Central Adirondacks, New York." In *Proterozoic Tectonic Evolution of the Grenville Orogen in North America*; eds. R. P. Tollo, L. Corriveau, J. McLelland, and M. J. Bartholomew, 325–36. *Geological Society of America Memoir* 197. Boulder, CO, 2004.

Darton, N. H. "The Mineralogical Localities in and around New York City, and the Minerals Occurring Therein." Supplement, *Scientific American* XIV, no. 344 (1882).

Darton, N. H., W. S. Bayley, R. D. Salisbury, and H. B. Kummel. *Geologic Atlas of the United States: Passiac Folio, New Jersey-New York.* Vol. 557. Washington, DC: US Geological Survey, 1908.

Domagala, M. A. and M. R. Selznick. *Paleontology and Stratigraphy of the Ledyard Shale (Middle Devonian) at Spring Creek, Alden, New York.* Rochester Academy of Science Mineral Section, Special Publication Series, no. 1 (1979).

Drury, George H., *The Historical Guide to North American Railroads: Histories, Figures, and Features of more than 160 Railroads Abandoned or Merged since 1930.* Waukesha, Wisconsin: Kalmbach Publishing, 1994.

Eckert, Allan W., *Earth Treasures Volume 1, The Northeastern Quadrant.* Lincoln, Nebraska: iUniverse, 2000.

Ehrets, J. R., "The West Fall (Upper Devonian Catskill Delta Complex: Stratigraphy, Environments, and Sedimentation." In *Field Trip Guide for the 53rd Annual Meeting of the New York State Geological Association,* 3–22. Binghamton, NY: SUNY, 1981.

Eldredge, Niles: "Systematics and Evolution of the Phacops Rana" (Green, 1832) and Phacops Iowensis (Delo, 1935) (Trilobita) from the Middle Devonian of North America." *Bulletin of the American Museum of Natural History* 147, Article 2 (1972).

Farthing, Dori, and Stephen Sidlaukas. *Slag from Standish, NY-A Boon or a Bane?* Paper presented at the annual meeting of the Geological Society of America, Philadelphia, PA: 22-25 (October, 2006).

Fisher, D. W. *Correlation of the Silurian Rocks in New York State*. New York State Museum and Science Service Map and Chart Series, 1959.

Fisher, D. W., Y. W. Isachsen, and L. V. Rickard. *Geologic Map of New York State, consisting of 5 sheets: Niagara, Finger Lakes, Hudson-Mohawk, Adirondack, and Lower Hudson*. New York State Museum and Science Service, Map and Chart Series, no. 15. 1970.

Gallagher, David. *Origin of the Magnetite Deposits at Lyon Mountain, N.Y.* New York State Museum Bulletin 311. Albany, NY, 1937.

Gates, A.E., D. W. Valentino, J. Chiarenzelli, M. Gorring, and M. Hamilton. "Field Trip to the Western Hudson Highlands." Paper presented at Long Island Geologists Conference, 2003.

Gillette, Tracy. *The Clinton of Western and Central New York*. New York State Museum Bulletin 341. Albany, NY, 1947.

Gooley, Lawrence P. *Lyon Mountain, the Tragedy of a Mining Town*. Peru, New York: Bloated Toe Publishing, 2004.

———. *Out of the Darkness, In Memory of Lyon Mountains Iron Men*. Peru, New York: Bloated Toe Publishing, 2005.

Gordon, J.S. "Sowing the American Dream." *American Heritage* 41, no. 8 (1990).

Grabau, A.W. *Geology and Paleontology of the Schoharie Valley*. New York State Museum Bulletin 92. Albany, NY, 1906.

Grasso, T.X. "Redefinition, Stratigraphy, and Depositional Environments of the Mottville Member (Hamilton Group) in Central and Eastern NY." In *Dynamic Stratigraphy and Depositional Environments of the Hamilton Group (Middle Devonian) in New York, Part 1*, 5–31. New York State Museum Bulletin 457. Albany, NY, 1986.

Hagni, R. D. "Titanium Occurrence and Distribution in the Magnetite-Hematite Deposit at Benson Mines, New York." *Economic Geology* 63 (1968): 151–55.

Hagni, R. D., R. A. Masiello, and P.H. Tumialan. 1969. "Metamorphic Aspects of the Magnetite-Hematite Deposit at Benson Mines, New York." *Economic Geology* 64 (1969): 183–90.

Hall, J., *Third Annual Report of the Fourth Geological District of the State of New York*. New York Geological Survey Annual Report 3 (1839): 287–339.

Hall, Russell. *Gem of the Adirondacks: Star Lake, Benson Mines & the Global Economy*. Florida: Lighthall Books, 2005

Halley, R. B. "Cryptalgal Limestones of the Hoyt (U. Cambrian) and Whitehall (U. Cambrian to L. Ordovician) Formations of New York State." *Geological Society of America Abstracts with Programs* 3, no. 1 (1971): 35.

Hawkins, Michael. "Ellenville, New York, a Classic Locality." *Rocks & Minerals* 82 (2007): 472–83.

Heckel, P.H. *Nature, Origin, and Significance of the Tully Limestone.* Geological Society of America Special Paper Series 138. 1973.

Herod, S. "NYCO Strengthens Operation with New Mine, Crushing Plant." *Pit & Quarry* (June 1984): 36–40.

Heyl, Allen V. "The Philips Mine: Another Perspective." *Matrix, A Journal of the History of Minerals* 5, no. 4 (Winter 1997).

Huddle, John W. and John E. Repetski. *Conodonts from the Genesee Formation in Western New York.* United States Geological Survey Professional Paper Series, 1032-B. 1981.

Isachsen, Y. W., E. Landing, J. M. Lauber, L. V. Rickard and W. B. Rogers, eds.. *Geology of New York, A Simplified Account.* New York State Museum Educational Leaflet 28. Albany, NY, 2000.

Jensen, David E. *Minerals of New York State.* Ward Press, 1978.

Kay, G.M. "Stratigraphy of the Trenton Group." *Geological Society of America Bulletin* 48, no. 1 (1937): 233–302.

Kearns, L.E. "The Amity Area, Orange County, New York." *Mineralogical Record* 9 (1978): 85–90.

Kemp, J. F. "Pyrrhotite Deposits at Anthony's Nose on the Hudson, N.Y." Transactions of the *American Institute of Mining Engineers.* (1894): 620.

Klemic, H., J. H. Eric, J. R. McNitt, and F. A. McKeown. *Uranium in Phillips Mine-Camp Smith Area, Putnam and Westchester Counties, New York.* United States Geological Survey Bulletin 1074-E. Washington, DC, 1959.

Lenik, E.J., *Iron Mine Trails.* New York-New Jersey Trail Conference: 1996.

Liebe, R. M., and T. X. Grasso. "The Devonian Stratigraphy of Cherry Valley, NY." *Northeastern Geology* 12, no. 1 (1990): 7–13.

Loveman, Michael H. "Geology of the Phillips Pyrites Mine Near Peekskill, New York." *Economic Geology* 6, no. 3, (1911): 235.

Lupulescu, M. "Minerals from New York State Pegmatites." *Rocks & Minerals* 82, no 6 (2007): 494–500.

Manchester, J.G. "The Minerals of New York City & Its Environs." *New York Mineralogical Club Bulletin* 3, no. 1 (1931): 95.

Mayer, Fritz. "Historic Mining Debris in Wurtsboro; Tailings Force Closure of State Land." *River Reporter* (Narrowsburg, New York), December 5, 2012.

McAlester, A. L. *Upper Devonian Pelecypods of the New York Chemung Stage.* Peabody Museum of Natural History Bulletin 16, 1962.

Miller, William J. "The Garnet Deposits of Warren County New York." *Economic Geology* 7, no. 5 (1912): 493–501.

Newland, David H. *The Mineral Resources of the State of New York*. New York State Museum Bulletin 223–224. Albany, NY, 1919.

———. *The Quarry Materials of New York: Granite, Gneiss, Trap Rock and Marble*. New York State Museum Bulletin 181. Albany, NY, 1916.

Newland, David H., and C. A. Hartnagel. *Iron Ores of the Clinton Formation in New York State*. New York Museum Bulletin 123. Albany, NY, 1908.

Oliver, Jr., W. A., and G. Klapper, G., eds. *Devonian Biostratigraphy of New York: Part 2, Stop Descriptions*. International Union of Geological Sciences, Subcommittee on Devonian Stratigraphy. Washington, DC: United States Geological Survey, 1981.

Palmer, D. F. "Geology and Ore Deposits near Benson Mines, New York." Economic Geology 65 (1970): 31–39.

Penfield Foundation. *Penfield Business History*. 2013. Copy at the Penfield Museum.

Penn, M. W. "Quartzite: Beauty, Strength, and Durability." *Building Stone Magazine* 32: no. 4 (Winter 2009): 18–21.

Peterson, Erich U., ed. *Selected Mineral Deposits of Vermont and the Adirondack Mountains, New York, I. Mineral Deposits of the Adirondack Mountains*. Guidebook Series 17. Littleton, CO: Society of Economic Geologists, 1993.

Reis, Heinrich. *The Geology of Orange County*. Geological Survey of New York, 454. 1895.

Richards, P. R. and G. W. Robinson. "Mineralogy of the Calcite-Fluorite Veins near Long Lake, New York." *Mineralogical Record* 31 (2000): 413–22.

Rickard, L. V. "The Middle Devonian Cherry Valley Limestone of Eastern New York." *American Journal of Science* 250 (1952): 511–22.

Rickard, L. V. Title unknown, in W. S. Cole, G. A. Cooper, and H. V. Owens, eds. *Field Trip Guide for the 27th Annual Meeting (30th anniversary) of the New York State Geological Association*. Hamilton, New York, 1955.

Robinson, G. W., and S. C. Chamberlain. "Gazetteer of major New York state mineral localities." *Rocks & Minerals* 82 (2007):472–83.

Rogers, William B., Yngvar W. Isachsen, Timothy D. Mock, and Richard E. Nyahay. *New York State Geological Highway Map*, Educational Leaflet 33. Albany, New York State Museum, 1990.

Rollins, H.B., N. Eldredge, and J. Spiller. 1971. *Gastropoda and Monoplacophora of the Solsville Member (Middle Devonian, Marcellus Formation) in the Chenango Valley, New York State.* Bulletin of the American Museum of Natural History 144: 131–70.

Ruedeman, R., and P. E. Raymond. *Paleontologic Contributions from the New York State Museum.* New York State Museum Bulletin 189. Albany, NY, 1916.

Shilling, Donovan A. "The Great Iron Ore Odyssey." *Crooked Lake Review* 124 (Summer 2002).

Sims, Paul K., and Preston E. Hotz. *Zinc-Lead Deposit at Shawangunk Mine, Sullivan County, New York.* United States Geological Survey Bulletin 978-D. 1951.

Sirkin, Les. *Eastern Long Island Geology with Field Trips.* Watch Hill, RI: Book and Tackle Shop, 1995.

———. *Western Long Island Geology with Field Trips.* Watch Hill, RI: Book and Tackle Shop, 1996.

Sorauf, J. E. "Upper Devonian (Frasnian) Rugose Corals from New York State." *Journal of Paleontology* 61, no. 4 (1987): 676–89.

Sorauf, J.E, and H. E. Roberson, H.E., "Upper Devonian Stratigraphy and Sedimentology in the Binghamton Area." In *Field Trip Guide for the 35th Annual Meeting of the New York State Geological Association,* 87–96. Binghamton, NY, 1963.

Stephenson, Robert C. *Titaniferous Magnetite Deposits of the Lake Sanford Area, New York.* New York State Museum Bulletin 340. Albany, New York, 1945.

Stoffer, Phil, and Messina, Paula. *Geology of the New York City Region.* USGS Educational Website, 2003.

Tan, Li-Ping. 1966. *Major Pegmatite Deposits of New York State.* New York State Museum and Science Service Bulletin 408. Albany, NY, 1966.

Tesmer, I. H. *Geology of Chautauqua County, New York: Part I. Stratigraphy and Paleontology (Upper Devonian).* New York State Museum Bulletin 391. Albany, NY. 1963.

Thibault, Newman W. "Celestite from Chittenango Falls, *New York.*" *American Mineralogist* 20, no. 3 (1035): 147–52.

Valentino, D., J. Chiarenzelli, D. Piaschyk, L. Williams, and R. Peterson. "The Southern Adirondack Sinitral Transpressive Shear System." In *Friends of the Grenville Field Trip Guidebook, Indian Lake, New York, Day 1, Saturday, September 27, 2008.*

Valley, J. W., E. J. Essene, and D. R. Peacor. "Fluorine-Bearing Garnets in Adirondack Calc-Silicates." *American Mineralogist* 68 (1983): 444–68.

Van Diver, Bradford B., *Roadside Geology of New York.* Roadside Geology Series. Missoula, MT: Mountain Press Publishing, 1985.

Ver Straeten, C.V., G. Baird, C. Brett, G. Lash, J. Over, C. Karaca, T. Jordan, and R. Blood. "The Marcellus Subgroup in Its Type Area, Finger Lakes Area of New York and Beyond." Chapter 3 in *Field Trip Guide for the 83rd Annual Meeting of the New York State Geological Association.* Syracuse, NY: Syracuse University, 2011.

Waite, Amanda, Victor P. Tollerton Jr., and Cynthia R. Domack. "A Paleontological Analysis of Middle Devonian Trilobites at the Cole Hill Roadcut in Madison County, New York." Paper 71-8, presented at the Northeastern Section (39th Annual) and Southeastern Section (53rd Annual) Joint Meeting of the Geological Society of America, March 25–27, 2004.

Walter, Michael. "Diamond Acres, Collect Stunning New York Quartz Crystals." *Rock & Gem Magazine* 34, no. 6 (2004).

Walter, Michael. "Ilion Gorge Travertine." *Rock & Gem Magazine* 34, no. 11 (2004).

Walter, Michael, and Steven C. Chamberlain. "Road-Cut Mineral Occurrences of St. Lawrence County, New York. Part 3: Oxbow Road Cut." *Rocks and Minerals* 84, no. 3 (2009).

Wilber, J. Scott. F. E., Mutschler, J. D. Friedman, and R. E. Zartman. "New Chemical, Isotopic, and Fluid Inclusion Data from Zinc-Lead-Copper Veins, Shawangunk Mountains, New York." *Economic Geology* 85 (1990):182–96.

Whitlock, H. P. *Minerals from Lyon Mountain, Clinton County.* New York State Museum Bulletin 107. Albany, NY, 1907.

Zabriskie, Dan and Carol. *Rockhounding in Eastern New York State and Nearby New England,* rev. ed. by Karl Hartkopf and Samantha Manburg. Albany, NY: Many Facets, 2006.

INDEX

ABOUT THE AUTHOR

Robert Beard is a geologist and has collected rocks for more than thirty years. In his early days of rock collecting, his colleagues said that he would get over the excitement of finding an interesting rock, but that never happened. He received his B.A. in geology, with a minor in mathematics, from California State University, Chico, in 1983, and his M.S. degree in geology from the University of New Mexico in 1987. He currently works in the environmental consulting industry as a geologist. He is a contributing editor to *Rock & Gem* magazine and has written for *Rock & Gem* since 1993. He currently lives in Harrisburg, Pennsylvania, with his wife, Rosalina, and children, Daniel and Roberta.